Daniel Henderson's new book, *Never Sh*  through the most difficult and perplexin

JIM CYMBALA | Senior Pastor of The Broc

Daniel Henderson has sought the face of God, found the heart of God, and then received from the hand of God for decades through his study, prayers, and applications of the Psalms. It is from this deep well of devotion that every single reader will benefit now in this thorough, masterful, and unavoidably practical engagement with Psalm 15. May all who read and receive this work be the Never Shaken for the glory of Christ.

ADAM BAILIE | Senior Lead Pastor of Christ Church, Gilbert, AZ

Daniel speaks to one of the most crucial needs of a Christian's heart-intimacy with God. A much-needed message in light of the turbulent days we are living in.

CHRISSY TOLEDO | Author, *Girl in the Song*

The world is filled with uncertainty and doubt. We need hope and steadfast faith, now more than ever. *Never Shaken* helps deliver that hope. An exposition of Psalm 15, the book was written as an overflow of Daniel Henderson's personal journey and passion for Christ. A resource every Christian needs, it will inspire, encourage, and equip you to live with victory in Jesus.

BRIAN BLOYE | Founding and Senior Pastor of West Ridge Church, Dallas, GA

During a time when my world was shaken to the core, Daniel Henderson stood by my side, pointed me to Scripture, and encouraged me to keep trusting God. In short, he embodied what this book is about for me! Daniel weaves together profound insights and personal experiences, inviting readers into a journey of unwavering trust in God. His words resonate with sincerity and biblical wisdom, traits born from years of pastoral service. This book is not just a good read, but a transformative experience that instills a sense of peace and strength for life's journey. This book is one of Daniel's most captivating and empowering books yet!"

JOSH WEIDMANN | Senior Pastor of Grace Chapel, Denver, CO

I don't know how many times I've read Psalm 15. But after reading *Never Shaken*, I won't read it the same again. With penetrating insight, vivid applications, and a pastoral heart, Daniel Henderson has written a profoundly insightful and encouraging book for a deeply disorienting age.

MARK VROEGOP | Lead Pastor, College Park Church in Indianapolis and author of *Dark Clouds, Deep Mercy*

Is victorious living possible? *Never Shaken* teaches you practical ways to experience greater intimacy with God and personal integrity in the midst of a culture of unmatched compromise. Everyone needs to read this life changing book that will help turn pain into purpose and leave a legacy of faith as you incorporate true worship into your daily life.

LINDA BARRICK | **Author and founder of Hope Out Loud**

In a world of increasing instability and anxiety, *Never Shaken* is a vital reminder of our unalterable foundation. Many people right now are distracted, disillusioned, and dejected. Daniel Henderson provides a prophetic call back to a life of purpose and power. What we do not need right now is more complexity and confusion. What we do need is a renewed and simple call to the person that God promises to bless. *Never Shaken* is that call. I am greatly encouraged by the timing of this book, and I eagerly recommend it.

ROBBIE SYMONS | **Lead Pastor of Preaching and Vision, Hope Bible Church – Oakville, Ontario**

So many pastors and leaders across our country look to Daniel Henderson for encouragement, for inspiration, for example. I count myself among those learners. Daniel is a pastor of pastors and a leader of leaders. For decades he has been a student of Psalm 15, a teacher of Psalm 15, a lover of Psalm 15. Most importantly, he has sought to live Psalm 15. Daniel, thank you for this labor of love in providing a fresh and penetrating look at this great psalm.

JEFF WELLS | **Senior Pastor of WoodsEdge Community Church, Spring, TX**

Daniel Henderson has been an inspiration to me for decades. As I read *Never Shaken* I became more excited about my walk with Jesus than ever before. With poignant stories, deep biblical truths, and fabulous humor, this is a resource for any Christian with a hunger to grow and to make an eternal difference! Daniel shows us how God knows best. We have to embrace, with passion, all that the Lord either brings our way or allows to come at us. Let's join Daniel in allowing the struggles of life to not only make us better, stronger people, but to empower us to live like Jesus!

KAREN COVELL | **Producer and Founding Director of The Hollywood Prayer Network**

NEVER SHAKEN

FINDING YOUR FOOTING
WHEN THE WORLD IS SLIDING AWAY

DANIEL HENDERSON

MOODY PUBLISHERS

CHICAGO

Edited by Connor Sterchi
Interior design: Ragont Design
Cover design: Faceout Studio, Spencer Fuller
Cover texture of gradient background copyright © 2023 by simplf/Shutterstock (2123458322). All rights reserved.
Author photo: Kelly Weaver Photography

ISBN: 978-0-8024-1694-0

Originally delivered by fleets of horse-drawn wagons, the affordable paperbacks from D. L. Moody's publishing house resourced the church and served everyday people. Now, after more than 125 years of publishing and ministry, Moody Publishers' mission remains the same—even if our delivery systems have changed a bit. For more information on other books (and resources) created from a biblical perspective, go to www.moodypublishers.com or write to:

Moody Publishers
820 N. LaSalle Boulevard
Chicago, IL 60610

1 3 5 7 9 10 8 6 4 2

Printed in the United States of America

To Jim and Cathy Maxim

With deepest appreciation for your never-shaken faith in Christ, love for one another (for almost 50 years), and service to the body of Christ. You have inspired countless lives to seek God and pray for their pastors. Jim, your friendship and support as board chairman has kept me in the fight more times than I can count.

AND

To Troy and Janel Keaton

With sincere admiration for your never-shaken trust in the goodness and grace of Christ as you have navigated life's difficult seasons with profound trust and genuine hope. Troy, as my pastor, you have inspired me week after week. Janel, your enduring faith through the cancer journey has adorned Christ so beautifully.

CONTENTS

Psalm 15

A Psalm of David.
O LORD, who may abide in Your tent?
Who may dwell on Your holy hill?
He who walks with integrity,
and works righteousness,
And speaks truth in his heart.
He does not slander with his tongue,
Nor does evil to his neighbor,
Nor takes up a reproach against his friend;
In whose eyes a reprobate is despised,
But who honors those who fear the LORD;
He swears to his own hurt and does not change;
He does not put out his money at interest,
Nor does he take a bribe against the innocent.
He who does these things will never be shaken.

STIRRED, NOT SHAKEN

Never Shaken:
Not disturbed from a firm position or state;
steadfast and unwavering.

"There are lots of nice things you can do with sand;
but do not try building a house on it."

C. S. Lewis

Paradise was flirting with disaster.

Hiking trails spanned the lush green miles like termite trails in an abandoned backcountry log home. Serene campsites hosted countless family memories every year. Flowing streams gently descended from the snow-capped crown of the massive peak into mighty rivers that provided hydroelectric energy to thousands. For hundreds of miles, the towering splendor was admired by airline passengers. Nearby, highway drivers rubbernecked at the sight. It was an outdoorsman's paradise and an unparalleled scenic wonder.

Then everything changed in just a few moments on May 18, 1980. The colossal Mount St. Helens, protruding 9,677 feet toward heaven and situated just fifty-two miles from Portland, Oregon, exploded in a cataclysmic event of unsettling destruction. The impact was felt all across North America. A magnitude 5.1 earthquake generated an immense collapse of the mountain's north face. It became the largest recorded debris avalanche in US history.[1]

Massive amounts of vegetation and buildings were destroyed

over a span of 230 square miles as 1.5 million metric tons of sulfur dioxide surged into the atmosphere. The destruction resulted in a crater almost two miles wide and a half-mile deep. The height of the mountain was condensed by some 1,300 feet.

In an instant, the force leveled much of the lush forest. Fifty-seven people perished. An estimated 7,000 big game deer, elk, and bear were killed along with approximately twelve million fish from a local hatchery. Two hundred homes were taken out. The intensity severely damaged 185 miles of highway and 15 miles of railways.[3]

A Riveting Reassurance

Some college friends and I visited the desolation just six weeks later. We drove spellbound along what had been the pristine Kalama River. Mile after mile of tree parts huddled together like boxes of randomly stacked toothpicks. The flowing ash annihilation had emptied the forest of all signs of life.

But there was one tree. A solitary survivor. Fixed in the very center of the ugly wilderness of what had once been a glorious river stood a deeply rooted rebel, announcing, "I'm still here!" It declared its presence like a beacon on the darkest coastline. The damaged limbs and lone trunk were still striving for existence following the torrent that annihilated so many of its living colleagues. This one had inexplicably beat the odds as a devastated mountain slid away.

Earlier that very morning, I read from Psalm 91:

A thousand may fall at your side, ten thousand at your right hand, but it will not come near you. You will only look with your eyes and see the recompense of the wicked. Because you have made the LORD your dwelling place—the Most High, who is my refuge. (Ps. 91:7–9 ESV)

Because you have made the LORD your dwelling place—
the Most High, who is my refuge—(Ps. 91:7–9 ESV)

I recorded this convergence of word and wonder in my journal. My heart said, "I want to be that tree, Lord. No matter what happens. Let me stand strong through the storms of life that invariably await me in this unpredictable journey called life."

Secure Through the Storms

The "eruptions" of our lives are real and often relentless. For me, events unfolded in the coming years that would pull at my roots and shake the branches of my ministry and family life. Waves of woundedness would soon slam into my pastoral soul and reverberate for decades.

Two leadership assignments involved stepping in as an "OSHA" pastor, assigned to post-disaster analysis and cleanup. I was tasked with picking up the heartbreaking aftermath of a predecessor's high-visibility moral failure. Like it or not, I became a personal target of those hurting people who hurt others—even their new leader.

An extended trial with a prodigal child would test the mettle of our parenting and marriage. Just as the economy was crashing in 2007–2008, I parachuted from the security of a megachurch, starting all over to launch a nonprofit prayer ministry. This risk would lead to a complete loss of all our accumulated home equity and months of scarcity and financial pressure as I tried to figure out how to raise funds with no congregation. Other difficulties have proved arduous.

Perhaps much harder challenges have invaded your comfort zone. The problems we all encounter are varied, but the nature of the testing is universally unsettling.

The image of that lone tree in a shattered panorama remains vivid in my mind even now. The illustration reminds me of the security that can be embraced by those who live by the gospel and walk authentically with God—especially in a world that often appears to be sliding away into an uncertain destination, much like a Mount St. Helens mountainside.

I find great comfort in the concluding promise of Psalm 15 that promises a never-shaken life. I am profoundly undergirded by a similar assurance from Jude: "Now to Him who is able to keep you from stumbling, and to make you stand in the presence of His glory blameless with great joy" (Jude 24).

Stirred, Not Shaken

James Bond, the British Secret Service agent in Ian Fleming's fictional book series, became notable for his stated preference for martini cocktails. If you are a 007 fan, you know it well: "Shaken, not stirred."[4]

But for those who follow Jesus, our stated testimony should be the opposite. "Stirred, not shaken." Yes, life will beat us up more than we might prefer. We may fail more than we wish. We may endure sickness, family conflict, financial pressures, job loss, and various shades of uncertainty—more than we think we can bear. But, because of the person and power of our living Christ, we may be *stirred but not shaken.*

BECAUSE OF THE PERSON AND POWER OF OUR LIVING CHRIST, WE MAY BE *STIRRED BUT NOT SHAKEN.*

But what do we mean by "stirred"? To stir is to excite strong feelings in someone or to rouse them from indifference.[5] While the unsettling realities of life can stir up deep emotions of fear, doubt, discouragement, and anxiety, we can also be stirred to more faithfully trust God's unchanging character. Stirred to embrace His truth. Stirred to cherish our essential relationships. Stirred to more resolutely live with integrity. Stirred to more boldly testify of His tailor-made grace. Indeed, stirred—not shaken.

God does not promise a smooth and stress-free life. Many of the most significant biblical characters and Christian heroes struggled with extraordinary afflictions. The Bible is real and raw about the sufferings of the Christ follower and goes to substantial lengths to warn us of the dangers of the comfort zone.

God knows that ease and prosperity can breed self-reliance and spiritual apathy. Abundance can fuel an independent spirit and neglect of the vital relationships we need with believers from all walks of life. The common mantra of "more" can lead to an unbridled appetite for accumulation, leading to blatant materialism and chronic dissatisfaction with life. So God, in His goodness, stirs us once again through unsettling experiences with the intention that the roots of our soul will grow deeper and the fruits of our testimony will flourish for His glory.

THE BIBLE IS BURSTING WITH PROMISES AND PROCLAMATIONS ABOUT THE UNSHAKABLE NATURE OF THOSE WHO GENUINELY KNOW GOD AND HAVE A VITAL RELATIONSHIP WITH THE ALMIGHTY.

Be encouraged. The Bible is bursting with promises and proclamations about the unshakable nature of those who genuinely know God and have a vital relationship with the Almighty. This book will conclude with powerful reassurances from God's Word for an unshaken life.

Proverbs contrasts the security of the righteous with the fragility of those who reject God.

- "A man will not be established by wickedness, but the root of the righteous *will not be moved.*" (Prov. 12:3)
- "When the whirlwind passes, the wicked is no more, but the *righteous has an everlasting foundation.*" (Prov. 10:25)
- "For a righteous man falls seven times, and *rises again,* but the wicked stumble in time of calamity." (Prov. 24:16)

We will encounter "whirlwinds" in life. Perhaps you feel like you are in one now. We will occasionally falter but will not ultimately fail.

The righteous rise in the strength and security of God's power. We do not have the assurance of an easy journey but can keep moving forward, with courage, in the hope of an eternally significant life. Our promised heavenly destiny makes this temporary earthly trek meaningful and missional.

Holding and Inhabiting

My wife, Rosemary, and I enjoy time with our eleven remarkable grandchildren. When walking alongside them, whether navigating a parking lot or hiking precarious terrain, we will grab their hand to provide safety and stability. Without the assurance of our grip, they inevitably would fall and scrape a knee or an elbow. But because we hold their hand, they do not tumble headlong into danger.

These little ones feel safe and are more secure because of the attentive care of someone bigger and stronger. It's the same way we are with God. David exclaimed, "My soul clings to You; Your right hand upholds me" (Ps. 63:8). In Psalm 16:8, David is under severe attack. He embraces the highest and best focus: "I have set the LORD continually before me; because He is at my right hand, *I will not be shake*n." He affirms the Lord's constant presence. He sets his heart on spiritual communion and the assurance of the Lord's strength at all times.

> OUR LIFE IS SOLID AND SECURE, NOT ONLY BECAUSE OUR GOD IS HOLDING OUR HAND, BUT BECAUSE HIS SPIRIT IS INHABITING OUR HEARTS.

Isaiah 41:13 assures, "For I am the LORD your God, who upholds your right hand, who says to you, 'Do not fear, I will help you.'" Jesus assures us, "I am with you always, even to the end of the age" (Matt. 28:20).

Even more assuring for us is the fact that our great God is not just *with* us, securing us by His almighty hand, but He is *in* us, and living *through* us in supernatural strength. Our life is solid and secure, not only because our God is holding our hand, but because His Spirit is inhabiting our hearts. "Greater is He who is *in* you than he who is in the world" (1 John 4:4). The Spirit who raised Christ from the dead indwells us to provide all we need in the hardest and most harrowing of times.

Solid Gospel Ground

Matthew's gospel account records Jesus' opening sermon of His public ministry on a mount near the Sea of Galilee. He shined the light of truth on people's choices about the foundation of their lives. He defined the fruits of genuine faith. He exposed the delusion of those who perform religious exploits but lack a sincere relationship with God through Christ. Finally, He spoke authoritatively about the folly of rejecting His gospel and, on the other hand, the security of obeying it. The final words of His life-altering sermon resound through the millennia:

"Therefore everyone who hears these words of Mine and acts on them, may be compared to a wise man who built his house on the rock. And the rain fell, and the floods came, and the winds blew and slammed against that house; and yet it did not fall, for it had been founded on the rock." (Matt. 7:24–25)

IT DOES NOT WORK TO UTILIZE GOD AS YOUR LIFE-PRESERVER IN DIFFICULT MOMENTS IF HE IS NOT YOUR VERY LIFE IN EVERY MOMENT.

God guarantees security and blessings to those who are in an authentic relationship with Him and who demonstrate faithful obedience. This person doesn't just affirm the truth but acts upon it. It is not their religious dogma, but their diligent doing that secures blessings. Trying harder to be a religious person is not enough. Nor does it work to utilize God as your life-preserver in difficult moments if He is not your very life in every moment.

The gospel's message is the exclusive pathway to ultimate security and strength in a world sliding away.

Sage Wisdom from a Satisfied Customer

Let's allow the story of one of the great biblical heroes to capture our hearts. David offers powerful testimony and practical truth to show us the pathway of an unshaken life, often during and after Mount St. Helens–like disruptions of life.

David's concluding line of Psalm 15 makes this promise: "He who does these things will never be shaken" (Ps. 15:5). He is sure of it. From his own unsettling experience of indescribable pain and uncertainty he remains clear and confident.

But take note: It does not say, "She who thinks about these things," or "He who reads about these things," or "She who believes these things." The point is clear: "He who *does* these things."

> TO BE OF VALUE, THIS BOOK MUST INSPIRE YOU TOWARD ACTION. IT IS A GUIDE TO PRACTICAL HABITS OF TRUST AND OBEDIENCE THAT MAKE FOR AN UNSHAKEN LIFE.

So, to be of value, this book must inspire you toward action. It is a guide to practical habits of trust and obedience that make for an unshaken life. More importantly, it must point you beyond David's words or mere human striving to focus your hope on the power of a living Christ who will work in you "both to will and to work for His good pleasure" (Phil. 2:13).

Let's discover His power and purpose to do this. One thing is sure. In these unsettling times, we need a life that is never shaken.

Chapter 1

THE STORIES OF OUR
UNSETTLED LIVES

I lay down and slept; I awoke, for the LORD sustains me.
I will not be afraid of ten thousands of people
Who have set themselves against me round about.

A Psalm of David, when he fled from Absalom his son.

PSALM 3:5–6

The conversion of a soul is the miracle of a moment;
the manufacture of a saint is the task of a lifetime.

ALAN REDPATH

The most influential person in government opened his press conference "with the suggestion that every newspaper in the country print the text of the Fifteenth Psalm." The passage had just been read at the services the renowned leader attended with his cabinet at St. John's Episcopal Church. He noted to the sea of reporters, "There could be no better lead for your story."[1]

So it was that the relevance of Psalm 15 captured President Franklin Delano Roosevelt's heart in a moment of extraordinary national and global crisis on March 5, 1938. It was the fifth anniversary of his first inauguration. The world was at the height of the Great Depression. The people of the United States were struggling to survive. Germany was on the march to dominate Europe. Just days later, Hitler invaded Austria. World War II loomed large. The fifteenth psalm had gripped Roosevelt's heart as prosperity and peace slid away. It still engages us today as we navigate a world that often feels as uncertain as sprinting in thick fog.

Never Shaken?

We struggle. We battle anxiety. Our body fails. Friends move away. We lose jobs. Coworkers scorn our faith. Our children walk away from the church.

Meanwhile, our prevailing culture has its feet firmly planted in midair as it assaults sensible morality and threatens our societal stability. We hold our breath waiting for a news report about the meltdown of another deranged shooter or the announcement of another global health crisis.

Can we really be unshaken? David, the author of Psalm 15, was a seasoned veteran of unsettling hardships. He had plenty of heartaches. David wrote prolifically with the praise that emerged from seasons of pain. He was no stranger to the long recovery road from tragic personal choices and agonizing family distresses. But over and over, he sang of the possibilities of an unshaken soul. David never wrote in a sterile vacuum of religious unreality. He wrote consistently and clearly from the crucible of a tested life.

Unsettled by Testing

The long road from David's early anointing as the future king of Israel to his eventual royal coronation was about as straightforward as San Francisco's famously winding Lombard Street. Scholars estimate a fifteen-year waiting period filled with dangers, toils, and snares. For agonizingly protracted years, he was a man on the run. The jealous and God-rejected King Saul resolved to erase David's influence and existence. David survived in caves, among the enemy camps of the

Philistines. He navigated the constant tension of wondering when the trials would end and his divine assignment would begin.

Unsettled by Personal Failure

David's greatness as the king of Israel took a hit in the coming years through scandalous sin. While relaxing on the palace rooftop as his troops were in battle, he caught a direct and extended gaze at beautiful Bathsheba bathing on a nearby rooftop. His lustful desire and unbridled sense of power led to personal disaster. He brought her into the palace for a passionate encounter. Then, to cover his sin, he arranged for the murder of her husband, a trusted military leader. David subsequently married the now-pregnant Bathsheba.

About a year later, the prophet Nathan confronted David. Filled with remorse, David repented, pleading with God for mercy. The illegitimately conceived child died soon after. The consequences of David's sin continued throughout the rest of his reign. His leadership and family life could easily be labeled as "sliding away" as he reaped the fruits of what he had previously sown.

Unsettled Again

Most of us hope that in our later years, the waters will calm and life will get steadier. We grow weary of disappointments, longing for better days. We yearn to finally clean up the messes hatched by our own unwise choices and the consequential unwise decisions of others. We often look forward to a greater sense of financial security. We speculate about a day when all the political, social, and moral upheaval will settle down. But, unfortunately, the harsh reality is that as long as we are on this earth, all that seems familiar and safe will likely keep sliding away.

Indeed, King David had similar hopes for a calmer life. Yet unfolding before him was one of the darkest chapters of his reign. His sincere confession and forgiveness before the prophet Nathan did not stop the harvest of consequences that would inevitably unfold. The ominous cloud of agonizing family drama cast a dark shadow over his later years. The summary of the last chapters of his life reads like a convoluted combination of murder mystery, family fracture, political coup, and public scandal.

An Unsettled Family and Future

Let's review the back story that will lead us to a deeper experience of Psalm 15. Approximately five years after David's fateful tryst with Bathsheba, his son Amnon raped his half-sister Tamar. David was in his midfifties at the time (2 Sam. 13:1–14). One cannot help but wonder if Amnon had adopted a similar behavior modeled by his dad with Bathsheba. "Take whatever you desire and deal with the repercussions later." To further compound the drama, David did little to deal with Amnon. The Bible only records that he felt angry (2 Sam. 13:21).

Two years later, Tamar's brother Absalom murdered Amnon (2 Sam. 13:28–30). No doubt he was seething with bitterness toward Amnon and deep frustration over the apathy of his father.

A three-year estrangement between Absalom and David followed as Absalom went into exile, staying with his maternal grandfather, a king in the land of Geshur (2 Sam. 13:38). No attempt at reconciliation was initiated by David during this time. The roots of resentment in Absalom's heart grew deeper.

At the urging of Joab, David's trusted general, the king allowed Absalom to return to reside in Jerusalem. Still, David refused to see him, insisting that Absalom live in his own separate house (2 Sam. 14:21–24, 28). The estrangement festered.

Assessing Absalom

At this point in the biblical narrative, we learn some basic facts about Absalom.

> Now in all Israel was no one as handsome as Absalom, so highly praised; from the sole of his foot to the crown of his head there was no defect in him. (2 Sam. 14:25)

You may remember that Absalom was known for his beautiful and bountiful hair (2 Sam. 14:26). (Incidentally, I am known for my lack thereof.) Absalom seemed unfamiliar with the concept of humility. He actually erected a monument to himself so that he would be remembered after his death (2 Sam. 18:18).

The toxic mix of pride, antipathy, discord, and ambition drove Absalom in the coming days as he made a dramatic daily arrival at the city gates of Jerusalem. Setting up his campaign headquarters, he intercepted all who came with a concern, posturing himself as the wise and caring judge while systematically demeaning King David. He steadily endeared the vulnerable citizens to a budding loyalty to himself.

Over time, he reached the desired outcome. The Bible states:

> In this manner, Absalom dealt with all Israel who came to the king for judgment; so Absalom stole away the hearts of the men of Israel. . . . And the conspiracy was strong, for the people increased continually with Absalom. Then a messenger came to David, saying, "The hearts of the men of Israel are with Absalom." (2 Sam. 15:6, 12–13)

David knew he had lost the allegiance of the majority of the people as they opted for the conspiring and ambitious son. Now in his midsixties, he faced another dramatic reversal in his journey.

David said to all his servants who were with him at Jerusalem, "Arise and let us flee, for otherwise none of us will escape from Absalom. Go in haste, or he will overtake us quickly and bring down calamity on us and strike the city with the edge of the sword." (2 Sam. 15:14)

Chuck Swindoll captures the moment well:

Just picture the scene. The once-great King David scrambling around, throwing a few things in a bag, preparing to flee from his own son. After all these years, once again he is running for his life. Surely, he recalled the years he lived like a fugitive while running from Saul. He's back at it. "Been there, done that!"[2]

Unsettled but Singing

In these circumstances, many might cope by resorting to drugs or alcohol. Anxiety, depression, anger, or revenge might consume others. It might be natural to wallow in self-pity, regurgitating all the mistakes of the past. Some may even consider taking their own life to escape the pain.

David sings!

His psalms are his songs, resonating in and through every circumstance. And yes, in Psalm 15, David sings. The early notes may have begun with dark, minor key reflection, but the psalm culminates with tones of undaunted assurance. His song lingered in Israel's worship as a plumb line of personal evaluation. So it remains today, in our treasury of the Psalms, as a roadmap for an unshaken soul.

The Setting of His Song

I believe David wrote Psalm 15 from this devastating but defining moment as he navigated his betrayal and banishment at the hands of his son Absalom. There is some fine detail here but stay with me. This will add compelling color and helpful context to our applications in the coming chapters.

Psalm 15 begins with two weighty questions. They serve as a time marker. David directs his song to God, referring in the same pen stroke to Yahweh's "tent" and His "holy hill." It reads, "O LORD, who may abide in Your tent? Who may dwell on Your holy hill?" (Ps. 15:1).

Commentators agree that this is a reference to the fact that the mobile tabernacle (tent) that housed the ark of the covenant was, at this point, relocated to a more permanent structure in Jerusalem—Zion, God's holy hill.

Prominent German scholars Carl Friedrich Keil and Franz Delitzsch conclude that this opening verse favors the time of David's exile at the hands of Absalom "when David was cut off from the sanctuary of his God, whilst it was in possession of men the very opposite of those described in this Psalm."[3]

Eugene Merrill, a distinguished professor of Semitics and Old Testament studies, reinforces this timing with a strong argument. Without getting into the weeds, he summarizes that the structure erected to house the ark of the covenant and the subsequent placing of the ark in Jerusalem occurred right at 977 BC. Absalom's rebellion then took place the following year (976 BC).[4]

The biblical account of this scene explains that as David was leaving Jerusalem, escaping Absalom's assault, the Levitical priests removed the ark of the covenant from the holy hill and brought it out to David on the edge of the city. David instructed them to take it back to Jerusalem where it had been, and still belonged (2 Sam. 15:25).[5] Again, this underscores the idea that the ark was lodged on the holy hill before Absalom's rebellion.

The Saga of an Unsettled Songwriter

Let's briefly revisit the biblical narrative as we bring this chapter to a close. We read in 2 Samuel 15:16–17, "So the king went out, and all his household after him. And the king left ten concubines to keep the house. And the king went out, and all the people after him. And they halted at the last house" (ESV).

David fled. He was going nowhere in particular, except away. As he went, he wondered. What would unfold next?

One biblical scholar explains:

> What emotion and pathos are woven into the fabric of those few words. David was leaving the great city of Zion—the city named after him, the City of David. As he came to the edge, at the last house, he stopped and looked back over the golden metropolis he had watched God build over the past years. His heart must have been broken as he stood there looking back, his mind flooded with memories. All around him the people of his household scurried past, leading beasts of burden piled high with belongings, running for their lives.[6]

ACHING PERPLEXITY PRODUCES WEIGHTY QUESTIONS. LIFE-CHANGING ANSWERS OFTEN EMERGE.

Perhaps it was at that last house that David paused to initiate his song. Aching perplexity produces weighty questions. Life-changing answers often emerge. Doubts may have tormented his soul. Under the inspiration of the Holy Spirit, David may have composed this masterpiece in a single sitting. Perhaps it took several days or weeks to discern the Lord's inspiration of the Psalm 15 truths. We do not know. But we know David would again find the grace and truth sufficient to embrace the promise of a never-shaken life. He would sing about it with confidence in His unshakable God.

Ever True and Timeless

In Israel's unfolding history, Psalm 15 would be recounted recurrently by pilgrims as they went to the temple to attend one of the great religious festivals. One of just two "entrance psalms" (along with Psalm 24), it became a liturgy for approaching God in corporate worship. These psalms typically involved a call and response (a question from the leader and an answer from the congregation). In this case, David asks the question. The Almighty provides profound and practical answers.

Whatever the case or context, this divinely inspired song remains true and timeless. In the ups and downs of David's life, the Holy Spirit sang in and through him. During the good and the bad, the terrific and the tragic, the Psalms flowed from David's heart and still speak to us today. They are our songs of celebration and consternation. They are our expressions of praise and pain. They nurture strength and security so that we might remain stirred but never shaken.

As is true in my experience, I assume you have days when the promise of an undaunted life feels rock solid under your feet.

> OUR LIVES CAN UNFOLD IN A STRANGE MIX OF MAGNIFICENCE AND MESS. OUR RELATIONSHIPS CAN BE DELIGHTFUL AND DREADFUL AT THE SAME TIME. OUR MISTAKES HAUNT US WHILE THE LESSONS HELP US. THROUGH IT ALL, WE NEED SECURITY AND STRENGTH.

Other days, this assurance might seem like sand on the beach sliding away under your feet as the waves retreat to the sea. The clouds of a heavy struggle can blur our perspective. But one thing is sure. We need to get back to the promise of Psalm 15:5: "He who does these things will never be shaken." So let us return there again—and again—with fresh resolve to renew our minds and reaffirm our obedience.

Loving and Living the Psalms

For decades, I met with a handful of church members early every Sunday morning to open a psalm and pray together. In those early Lord's Day moments, we would linger in each psalm for thirty minutes, even up to an hour. We journeyed through the Psalter five times over those years. Today, my ministry, Strategic Renewal, has produced a commentary and prayer guide for every one of the Psalms, entitled *Praying the Psalms.*[7]

I have fallen in love with the Psalms. I love leading prayer experiences with their truth shaping my praise, confession, requests, and preparation for the day. Psalm 15 has become my favorite of them all. In the coming pages, we will indeed linger on Psalm 15. Each chapter will include a "Never Shaken Application."

Like David, our lives can unfold in a strange mix of magnificence and mess. Our relationships can be delightful and dreadful at the same time. Our mistakes haunt us while the lessons help us. Through it all, we need security and strength. The same God who carried David to that place and provided all he needed for an unshaken life will do the same for you.

Never Shaken Application

- Take a moment to recall one of the most difficult chapters of your life. Was there a particular psalm or passage of Scripture that God used to sustain your soul? If so, which one was it and how did it shape your perspective?
- Think of another favorite psalm you have loved throughout your spiritual journey. Take a moment to read it again now. Get creative and put some musical notes to it, perhaps borrowing

the melody of some familiar tune. Sing it to the Lord, and to your own soul, to experience the help and reassurance you may need, even now.

• Read Psalm 15 aloud (whether alone or in a group), keeping in mind the grim experience that likely inspired this song. Then, make a commitment to memorize Psalm 15 so that you can meditate on its truths to strengthen your soul in the coming weeks.

Chapter 2

OUR QUEST STARTS WITH QUESTIONS

O LORD, who may abide in Your tent?
Who may dwell on Your holy hill?

PSALM 15:1

What is the only sure test by which the world will know who are
the real worshipers of the true God and who are just pretending?
Answer: loss and suffering. The only sure test is to strip from
worshipers something of value, and then we shall see if they really
worship the living God and bow down to him simply because he is
God. Only when worship comes at a cost may we tell if it is true.
Suffering is the fire that refines and reveals the heart of worship.

CHRISTOPHER ASH

Inquiring minds want to know. Unsettled souls wish to understand. Earnest souls choose to seek.

From the time humans perceived the world around them and could process words, we asked questions. It's part of having a soul. We are made in the image of God—not just as physical and emotional creatures, but also spiritual ones.

Biblical history demonstrates the power of questions. Satan used a question to prompt doubt and deception in Eve. After the fall, God asked Adam four questions to expose the situation and incite Adam toward honest admission of his sin. When Cain killed his brother,

Abel, God approached him with two questions. Jesus demonstrated the sway of questions throughout His earthly ministry to prompt gospel conversation, provoke more profound thought, bring conviction, and baffle His opponents.

Questions: Early and Eternal

Child development experts claim that at between twenty-one and twenty-four months, young children begin to ask, "What's that?" (Or simply "Dat?") Between twenty-six and forty months, they ask "Where?" and "Who?" questions. A few months later, they begin to ask "Is . . . ?" and "Do . . . ?" questions. At forty-two months and beyond, they ask "when, why, and how" questions.

We spend almost daily time with our youngest grandson, Eli. At just twenty-five months, he asks "Why?" at least two dozen times a day. He is pretty advanced for his age. But his curiosity (and, in some cases, toddler rebellion) drives him to get an answer to this fundamental question of human existence and, on occasion, drives his parents crazy.

A study in the United Kingdom found that, on average, children ask their parents seventy-three questions daily.[1] No wonder moms and dads are stressed and overwhelmed. According to the following survey of 1,500 parents, the top ten questions children ask their parents are:

1. Why do people die?
2. Where did I come from?
3. What is God?
4. How was I made?
5. What does "We can't afford it" mean?
6. Is Father Christmas real?
7. Why do I have to go to school?
8. When you die, who will I live with?

9. Why is the sky blue?

10. Why can't I stay up as late as you?[2]

As we mature in life, our questions may be less frequent, but they become more complicated. The actual words certainly change, but the longings that give birth to our questions remain.

In truth, we can never stop asking questions because our pursuit of truth (not just superficial answers) has been implanted in us by God. Writers on the topic observe that our questions foster personal growth, spark creativity, make us more empathetic, keep us young, and encourage humility.[3] Arguably, the day we stop asking questions is the day we stop growing.

As image bearers of God, because we are searching for meaning, yearning for truth, and longing for a purpose, we ask questions. He made us to do so. We are wise to do so. We must do so if we are to learn and grow.

Psalm 15 begins with two penetrating and pertinent questions. They are two sides of the same coin of inquiry: "O LORD, who may abide in Your tent? Who may dwell on Your holy hill?"

The Ultimate Questions for an Unshaken Life

To review, David was at a low point in the golden years of his life. He was betrayed and banished. Heartbroken and homeless. Unsettled and uncertain. He was sidelined and suffering. He was banished to the wilderness of Gilead while fickle traitors and hypocritical pretenders commandeered Israel's religious center. Imagine the questions that would explode in the human soul at a time like this. Maybe, in this moment, the dark curiosity of your heart is yearning for answers too.

Like all of us, David could have asked a series of common questions.

- Why did this happen?
- Why didn't I see this coming?
- What will I do now?
- How can I recover from this?
- When will this dark moment end?

And, right now, in the unsettledness of your life, you might be asking a set of your own questions:

- Why can't I get my act together?
- Where will I get a job?
- Will my marriage ever get better?
- Will I ever feel healthy again?
- Will I ever marry—or have children?
- Will my children turn out okay?
- Will our country ever turn around again?

But David really had one paramount question. It was a multifaceted "Who?" question. His inquiry centered in the character of God and the characteristics of those who truly know Him.

David had learned through the experience of his perplexing life to ask the right questions to center his heart on the core issues. He was determined to grow through the pain. No excuses. No rabbit trails of mere human reason. Just the highest and best answers from almighty God, springing from a clear and compelling hunger.

Asking a True and Trusted Source

David directs his question to Yahweh—the eternal, self-existent, covenant-keeping God. He was the only rock that wasn't rolling in his life. And, for an inquiry of life-altering magnitude, David knew he must get his answers directly from above. All the while, the scene was swirling with human opinion and contradictory reports.

The same is true today. Where do you seek answers when you need strength for a tough day? Who will you call to help you navigate this maze of life that leaves you unsure and insecure? An opinion poll of your network of friends might leave you more confused than a goat on artificial turf. Social media can provide endless and contradictory theories. Suppose you trust your emotions or subjective thoughts in a moment of crisis. In that case, you might dig the ditch of confusion deeper than the foundation trenches of your new home. Your "inner voice" can be as fallible as bombastic headlines from the latest edition of *The National Enquirer* tabloid.

> **DURING UNSETTLING TIMES, WE NEED INSIGHT FROM THE WORD, NOT THE WORLD. WE NEED ANSWERS FROM GOD, NOT OUR "GUT."**

During unsettling times, we need insight from the Word, not the world. We need answers from God, not our "gut." Our clarity and confidence must be rooted in the soundness of Scripture, not the subjectivity of society. David chose to go to God first in honesty and humility.

Answers That Affirm and Assure

In verse 1, David raises the issue of spiritual authenticity in a world of prevailing religious pretense. The cunning conspirators had hijacked the holy hill and were now in charge of "worship." David, a banished king, was hunkered down in some distant dirt—unsure about the past, unsettled in the present, and uncertain of his future. He was physically expelled from the center of Israel's worship. Still, he determined to center his heart in the reality of intimacy with all-present Yahweh, whose power and presence could not be contained in just one location.

Perhaps he was feeling insecure about his own standing with God after all the mistakes of his life. Maybe he just needed a reassuring refresher on the nature of true faith because a lot of fakery was floating around. When the priest brought the ark of the covenant to him on the outskirts of town, David reflected, "Return the ark of God to the city. If I find favor in the sight of the LORD, then He will bring me back again and show me both it and His habitation. But if He should say thus, 'I have no delight in you,' behold, here I am, let Him do to me as seems good to Him" (2 Sam. 15:25–26). Translation: "I am submitting to God's assessment of me now. If He delights in me, I will return to Jerusalem to worship there. If not, I will submit to His will."

David's questions cut to the core of our modern-day search for spiritual clarity. The answers he affirmed in Psalm 15 guide us to evaluate our walk with Christ. David's journey leads us to fruitful abiding and unshaken assurance.

He queries, "Oh LORD, who may abide in Your tent?" To *abide* means to sojourn. In this earthly realm's temporary "vapor," an individual can have an assured audience with the eternal God. While we all wander on this earth for a short time, some can know the wonder of everlasting intimacy with Yahweh. But who is it who can draw near to God? Who enjoys His presence? Who is the genuine worshiper?

In an immediate follow-up, David ponders, "Who may dwell in Your holy hill?" To *dwell* is to feel at home. No pretense. No discomfort. No doubting. A sense of true belonging in the presence of the Almighty—welcomed by Him, accepted by Him. Secure and safe in His strong arms.

The Best of Songs in the Worst of Times

Scholars propose that during this same period of exile, David or his associates (known as the sons of Korah) wrote other psalms that echo themes of this banishment and yearning for the holy hill.[4] They reflect a deep longing for intimacy with the Almighty, a hopeful return to the place of His dwelling, and a needed reassurance during these uncertain moments of displacement. Notice some of the key themes in the other songs that God inspired:

But know that the LORD has set apart the godly man for
Himself; the LORD hears when I call to Him. . . . Many are
saying, "Who will show us any good?" Lift up the light of
Your countenance upon us, O LORD! (Ps. 4:3, 6)

But as for me, by Your abundant lovingkindness I will enter
Your house, at Your holy temple I will bow in reverence for You.
O LORD, lead me in Your righteousness because of my foes; make
Your way straight before me. . . . But let all who take refuge in
You be glad, let them ever sing for joy; and may You shelter them,
that those who love Your name may exult in You. (Ps. 5:7–8, 11)

O LORD, I love the habitation of Your house and the place
where Your glory dwells. Do not take my soul away along
with sinners, nor my life with men of bloodshed. (Ps. 26:8–9)

One thing I have asked from the LORD, that I shall seek:
That I may dwell in the house of the LORD all the days of my
life, to behold the beauty of the LORD and to meditate in His
temple. (Ps. 27:4)

As the deer pants for the water brooks, so my soul pants for
You, O God. My soul thirsts for God, for the living God;
when shall I come and appear before God? (Ps. 42:1–2)

O send out Your light and Your truth, let them lead me; let
them bring me to Your holy hill and to Your dwelling places.
(Ps. 43:3)

Confuse, O Lord, divide their tongues, for I have seen
violence and strife in the city. Day and night they go around
her upon her walls, and iniquity and mischief are in her
midst. Destruction is in her midst; oppression and deceit do

not depart from her streets. . . . We who had sweet fellow-
ship together walked in the house of God in the throng. . . .
As for me, I shall call upon God, and the LORD will save me.
(Ps. 55:9–11, 14, 16)

O God, You are my God; I shall seek You earnestly; my soul
thirsts for You, my flesh yearns for You, in a dry and weary
land where there is no water. Thus I have seen You in the
sanctuary, to see Your power and Your glory. (Ps. 63:1–2)

Scholars Keil and Delitzsch even propose that Psalm 23 was written at this time of David's later-in-life exile.[5]

He restores my soul; He guides me in the paths of righteousness for His name's sake. Even though I walk through the
valley of the shadow of death, I fear no evil, for You are with
me. . . . Surely goodness and lovingkindness will follow me
all the days of my life, and I will dwell in the house of the
LORD forever. (Ps. 23:3, 4, 6)

The same scholars place another well-known psalm at this same
moment in David's life.[6]

My soul longed and even yearned for the courts of the LORD;
my heart and my flesh sing for joy to the living God. . . .
For a day in Your courts is better than a thousand outside. I
would rather stand at the threshold of the house of my God
than dwell in the tents of wickedness. (Ps. 84:2, 10)

Christopher Ash has noted, "It is loss that reveals the true worshiper
and separates the fair-weather Christian from the true worshiper."[7] In
his later years, David is facing the loss of all the external trappings that
defined his life and kingly reign. Once again, David shows why he is

a "man after [God's] own heart" (1 Sam. 13:14). His deepest longing is not for retribution or the recovery of power. Instead, his desire is for God Himself.

Our Pursuit of Privilege and Presence

We all love to experience a close encounter of a personal kind with an individual of great prominence. Some people eagerly pay big bucks for a ringside chair at an MMA fight, a front-row seat at a concert, or a privileged table at a political fundraiser.

I've had a few of these experiences in my journey. They were all free to me but fun and fulfilling. As a seminary student, I was honored to sit one-on-one in the offices of some notable preachers for a research project—men like Vance Havner, W. A. Criswell, Charles Stanley, Chuck Smith, Robert Schuller, Rex Humbard, and E. V. Hill. I've shaken hands and engaged in brief conversation with a couple of US presidents. As a pastor in California, I participated in a private lunch with three other community leaders as we hosted Billy Graham before his crusade in our city. I have the joy of being personal friends with several well-known pastors whose names you would likely recognize.

I suspect you've had encounters like this as well. Perhaps some more notable. We all cherish up-close-and-personal time with a distinguished person. But no human-to-human interchange compares to the privilege contemplated in Psalm 15:1: "O LORD, who may abide in Your tent? Who may dwell on Your holy hill?" Eugene Peterson interprets

> SPIRITUAL PURSUIT AND PASSION INSPIRED AN UNWORTHY KING TO CONTEMPLATE THE WONDER OF AN EVER-WORTHY GOD. HIS INQUIRY LED HIM BACK TO THE PROMISE OF AN UNSHAKEN LIFE AT A MOMENT WHEN HE NEEDED IT MOST.

it this way: "GOD, who gets invited to dinner at your place? How do we get on your guest list?" (MSG).

Interpersonal interactions with presidents, politicians, and preachers pale in comparison to an intimate encounter and an authentic relationship with the almighty God. Spiritual pursuit and passion inspired an unworthy king to contemplate the wonder of an ever-worthy God. His inquiry led him back to the promise of an unshaken life at a moment when he needed it most.

Character: Real and Revealed

As noted in the previous chapter, this psalm would have been considered later in Israel as an "entrance" psalm where "worshipers inquire of the priest as to the qualifications of admission to the holy place" and "the priest responds by specifying the requirements... and concludes with a blessing."[8] Psalm 15 delineates requirements, viewed by Old Testament scholars as a set of "ten commandments."[9] The Talmud, an ancient Jewish commentary, concluded, "Of the 613 commandments of the Pentateuch, each is summarized in this Psalm."[10] The fifteenth Psalm is the Old Testament standard of authentic faith.

For Christians, these qualities define the outliving character of the indwelling Christ. As New Testament believers, we understand that Psalm 15 is not a list of conditions for those who hope to be saved. Rather, it is a description of the character of those who are. Through a gospel lens, we realize that Psalm 15 is not about the means of salvation but the marks of salvation. Living in the assurance of this life-changing faith brings true security and strength.

Today, we might ask the question differently: "Lord, who really has eternal life on this temporary earth?" or "Lord, who authentically abides in Christ? What will their life look like?"

This is significant for us today because the church and the kingdom of heaven are described as a field with "tares among wheat" (Matt. 13:24–30). Not everyone who looks like a Christian, or talks like a Christian, is a Christian. Jesus taught that many who appeared on this planet as all-star spiritual performers would be in for the surprise of their eternal destiny when they stand before Him—because He "never knew them" in actual experience (Matt. 7:21–23). Although they professed "Lord, Lord" and did many impressive works, they did not do His will. They lacked a genuine relationship. John Calvin wrote, "Nothing is more common in the world than falsely to assume the name of God, or to pretend to be his people."[11] There is a difference between those who seek strength and security in religious duty or moral behavior and those who experience these realities in a daily relationship with God through Christ.

Jesus declared, "You will know them by their fruits" (Matt. 7:20). Adopting a Christian label is not evidence of spiritual life. Attending religious events does not produce a regenerated heart. Just as peaches grow on a peach tree and grapes emerge from a grapevine, the traits of Psalm 15 demonstrate an authentic faith, especially in a world that seems to be sliding into confusion about the true nature of Christian character.

Psalm 15 assures us of a healthy and secure life of demonstrated discipleship. It calls us to a consistent testimony of integrity at several levels. It compels us to allow the power of Jesus' life to work in us to manifest the fruit of His never-shaken life in everything we do. For the Christ follower, the promise is real: "For it is God who is at work in you, both to will and to work for His good pleasure" (Phil. 2:13).

The Questions That Count

Yes, your children may ask you seventy-three questions a day. As tiresome as that can be, you still delight in knowing that your kids are at least curious. Children are driven to learn. They need answers that will help them find meaning in this life and mature into healthy adults.

In our longing to experience an unshaken life, we may need to again become like a little child. Ask questions. Ask the right questions. Ask the core questions. Rekindle a holy curiosity.

- Lord, is my faith authentic?
- If my walk with You is real, how will it be evident to others?
- How will I trust Christ to produce this kind of unshaken character in me?

In a world of diluted devotion and confused definitions of "Christian," Psalm 15 brings clarity. In these unsettling times that threaten to shake us to the core, we can rediscover the anchors of truth to bring security and strength. David needed this. We need it. God provides it to all who will ask.

Never Shaken Application

- What questions are you asking of the Lord in this season of life? What do these questions reveal about your deepest heart desires? How will you surrender those desires to the Lord today?
- When have you been in the presence of some notable or famous person? Who was it, and what was the situation? How does their fame and influence compare to the person and presence of almighty God? How can this realization motivate you to seek God more diligently?
- As you review the "fruit" of authentic faith described in Psalm 15, which character quality do you most need the Lord to produce in you, by His grace, right now? How did Christ model this quality in His earthly ministry? Trust Him to work in you to shape this reality in your heart today.

Chapter 3

STRAW, STICKS, AND SOLID BRICKS

He who walks with integrity, and works righteousness,
And speaks truth in his heart.

PSALM 15:2

Integrity is like the weather: everybody talks about it
but nobody knows what to do about it.

STEPHEN L. CARTER

Who can forget the childhood emotion of hearing the hungry and horrifying big bad wolf exclaim, "I'll huff. And I'll puff. And I'll blow your house down!"? Even in our youngest memories, we all secretly hoped that our house would stand the assault of the carnivorous canine. But, as we know, two of the three little pigs almost became fresh bacon for the ravaging attacker.

The story of "The Three Little Pigs," made famous in the world of English fairy tales, illustrates the importance of the reliability of our choices. Even little pigs must be sure of the integrity of their homes and the strength of the material they use to build them.

As you likely remember, mama pig booted her offspring into the world to survive independently. The first little pig was quite lazy. He hurriedly built his house with straw. Piggy number two, also a bit negligent and in a hurry to have some fun, settled for sticks.

Finally, the industrious third pig chose to labor on until he had a solid brick dwelling.

The straw and sticks were no competition for the force of the wolf's windy assault. Pigs one and two, suddenly homeless, fled to their sibling's solid structure. All three eventually survived the assault in the security of the brick house. The wolf met his demise by slinking down the chimney of house #3 right into a pot of boiling water. Thanks to the bricks' stability, the menacing wolf became a tasty meal for the little swine (assuming cooked wolf meat can be delicious)— and they all lived happily ever after.

Start Here: Integrity

Breaches of integrity had peppered David's misguided choices in recent years (adultery, murder, parental neglect). He knew the painful price tag of settling for straw and sticks in matters of personal behavior. David now composes this song of reflection while navigating painful rejection and isolation. His son Absalom has thrown integrity to the wind and forced his royal father into oblivion. In his wilderness moment, David underscored the importance of bricks. Perhaps he is sensing the wolflike, internal threats of anger, compromise, revenge, or despondency huff and puff upon his beleaguered heart.

God inspires David to start this affirmation of these characteristics of the godly with the essential truth of integrity. In answer to David's inquiring tune about the marks of those who know and experience God's presence, the Holy Spirit imparts the first and primary quality: "He . . . walks with integrity."

David sang his opening lines about the kind of integrity that is woven into all matters of behavior and motive. He will portray how it shows up in the varied nuances of our relationships. Integrity in one's finances even makes the list. God expected and would empower David to fit the pieces of his broken life together again in a recommitment to undisputable integrity, and He expects the same of you and me.

Acute Integrity Deficiency Syndrome

We all have heard of or personally known those who have been affected by the Acquired Immunodeficiency Syndrome (AIDS) virus. But a different kind of "AIDS" destroys millions of lives, marriages, friendships, careers, companies, political aspirations, and Christian ministries every year: Acute Integrity Deficiency Syndrome. We've come a long way from the fabled days of the boy George Washington cutting down the cherry tree. The young future president told his father, "I cannot tell a lie." Today it seems many cannot tell the truth, and most cannot tell the difference.

We can identify with David's cry, "Help, LORD, for the godly man ceases to be, for the faithful disappear from among the sons of men. They speak falsehood to one another; with flattering lips and with a double heart they speak" (Ps. 12:1–2).

There is no laboratory-produced antidote or cure for this integrity deficiency. Only a transformation of the mind, a conversion of the heart, a setting of the will, and a consistent reception of divine grace can heal this deficiency.

Clarifying Integrity

"Integrity" in Psalm 15:2 (also translated "blameless" or "honest") implies what is whole, or wholehearted, and sound.[1] The Hebrew (*tāmîm*), appearing approximately fifty times in the Hebrew Bible, literally means complete, sincere, or perfect.[2]

The Latin root is *integer.* So a person of integrity is a whole person—a person undivided. All the pieces fit together into a whole. "The word conveys not so much a single-mindedness as a completeness; not the frenzy of a fanatic who wants to remake all the world in a single mold but the serenity of a person who is confident in the knowledge that he or she is living rightly."[3]

To "walk" in integrity is not a matter of putting one foot in front of the other. Instead, this is a reference to a consistent pattern of living. Billy Graham aptly noted, "Integrity is the glue that holds our way of life together."[4]

Know, Grow, Show

Author Stephen Carter proposes that integrity requires three things: (1) Discerning what is right and what is wrong; (2) Acting on what you have discerned, even at personal cost; and (3) Saying openly that you are acting on your understanding of right from wrong.[5] Borrowing from Carter, I have summarized integrity similarly as the commitment to KNOW, GROW, and SHOW.

KNOW the Truth

The very first psalm sets the foundation for a walk of integrity: "How blessed is the man who does not walk in the counsel of the wicked, nor stand in the path of sinners, nor sit in the seat of scoffers! But his delight is in the law of the LORD, and in His law he meditates day and night" (Ps. 1:1–2).

Integrity is based on understanding what is right and wrong, and this clarity springs from a longing for and delight in the regular intake of the Scriptures. To desire to grow in integrity but to neglect the Bible is to dream of "brick" but to build with straw and sticks.

We choose integrity every day by "taking heed" of the Word. "How can a young man keep his way pure? By keeping it according to Your word. With all my heart I have sought You; do not let me wander from Your commandments. Your word I have treasured in my heart, that I may not sin against You" (Ps. 119:9–11).

The constant daily onslaught of deception and degradation demands that we firmly remain unaltered by the world around us. The

Bible is the influence for this resolve toward integrity. "And do not be conformed to this world, but be transformed by the renewing of your mind, so that you may prove what the will of God is, that which is good and acceptable and perfect" (Rom. 12:2).

GROW in the Truth

At the same time, we must act on what we have discerned with daily resolve and painstaking attentiveness. Unfortunately, the world, our flesh, and the devil offer numerous alternatives to integrity. Here are three common pitfalls we must avoid as we grow in the truthfulness of integrity.

1. Refusing Pragmatism

The mantra of a pragmatist is "whatever works." In essence, the end justifies the means. As long as it turns out okay, it does not matter if there are shades of compromise in getting there. But the truth is not defined by our experiences or our opinions. Our tainted perspective can lead us to negotiate on principle in the process—as long as we get the desired product. A pleasing outcome or some sense of personal benefit does not define what is biblically correct.

> INTEGRITY REQUIRES THAT THE "BACKSTAGE" OF OUR AUTHENTICITY IS CONSISTENT WITH THE "FRONTSTAGE" OF OUR APPEARANCE.

2. Rejecting Hypocrisy

Integrity requires us to sniff out and snuff out all trappings of hypocrisy. In ancient Greece, a *hupokrites* was an actor in a play who wore a mask to fulfill his role in the drama. It came to refer to anyone who pretends to be someone they are not. We must seek to discard the public masks that can eventually accommodate our duplicity.

You've likely heard that integrity is who we are when no one is watching. The God who sees is the One we seek to please through a life of true integrity. Integrity requires that the "backstage" of our authenticity is consistent with the "frontstage" of our appearance. The theory of our day emphasizes that it doesn't matter what you do in your private life as long as your public life doesn't disrupt society. Quoting Billy Graham again, "Integrity means that if our private life was suddenly exposed, we'd have no reason to be ashamed or embarrassed. Integrity means our outward life is consistent with our inner convictions."[6] Jesus warned His followers to avoid the hypocrisy of the religious leaders of His day: "Do not do according to their deeds; for they say things and do not do them" (Matt. 23:3).

3. Shunning Compartmentalization

If integrity is a life where all the pieces fit together, then its antithesis is compartmentalization. Compartmentalization is "a defense mechanism in which thoughts and feelings that seem to conflict or to be incompatible are isolated from each other."[7] It involves actions that are clearly wrong in one area of life but, in the mind, are "separated" (kept secret) in order to deny the conviction of the Spirit and avoid getting caught. Walls rather than wholeness are the modus operandi.

In two of my pastoral assignments, I was called to succeed former senior pastors who had been exposed in moral failure and forced to resign. In one case, the church leader carried his secrets for almost eight years. The hurting members left affected by the fallout often asked me how he could have kept preaching, marrying people, baptizing new converts, and leading some semblance of a normal family life. Compartmentalization was evidently the coping mechanism. In varying degrees, any one of us could be tempted to manage our lack of integrity the same way.

A newspaper story appeared some years ago about a young man in Long Beach who went into a KFC to get some chicken for himself and his female companion. While she waited in the car, he went in to pick up the chicken. The store manager accidentally handed the guy the box in which he had placed the money from the daily sales. He put the money in a fried chicken box to conceal the large deposit.

The customer took the box back to the car and went on his way. They went to a nearby park to enjoy the chicken only to discover they had a box full of money. Realizing the mistake, they had a stroke of honesty and returned to the KFC. The manager was elated and relieved! He was so impressed that he asked the young customer to stick around, noting, "I want to call the newspaper and have them take your picture. You're the most honest guy in town."

"Oh, no, don't do that!" said the trustworthy customer.

"Why not?" asked the manager.

"Well," he said, "you see, I'm married, and the woman I'm with is not my wife."[8]

A person of integrity fights compartmentalization. He is integrated and authentic. There is no duplicity of attitudes and actions.

SHOW the Truth

We live out integrity with unambiguous declarations of our intentions. This public commitment reinforces accountability and strengthens our intended testimony.

I fashioned twelve family principles for my children as they were growing up. I hoped they would embrace them in life. We reviewed them regularly. I gave them a personalized notebook as a keepsake. They still have some of the Henderson Family Values memorized and, in various forms, they pass them on to their children.

My public articulation of these gave my kids frequent opportunities to reinforce them in my own life and parenting. One of them was, "Pray and read your Bible every day." They watched to see if I did it. Another was, "Always keep your word." They enthusiastically reminded me of my declaration whenever I told them I would do something.

The Pathway Toward Integrity

Integrity demands that we carefully incorporate truth, keep an unwavering commitment, and portray an authentic testimony into the fabric of everyday life. This is a vital recipe for integrity but one we must carefully steward.

My favorite dessert is crème brûlée (my wife makes a delectable one). It is a baked dessert custard with a sweet caramelized top. The simple ingredients include egg yolks, sugar, and heavy cream, with a topping of burnt brown sugar. What's not to like? Yet the process is precise. You cannot just throw the ingredients in a big bowl, shake them together and eat it. Instead, the recipe outlines a specific process of mixing, heating, cooling, baking, and cooling again. The final top coat of caramelized brown sugar adds a crunchy, finishing touch.

Integrity is not complicated, but it cannot be careless. It requires great intentionality and watchfulness.

The Gospel Empowerment

Our ultimate example of integrity is Jesus Christ. Hebrews 4:15 tells us, "For we do not have a high priest who cannot sympathize with our weaknesses, but One who has been tempted in all things as we are, yet without sin." He understands our fight for integrity. He bids us to come to Him in the battle to receive His grace to live blamelessly. He lives in us and through us to impart a supernatural capacity for a lifestyle of integrity.

Paul demonstrated the power of Christ to forge a blameless life. He testified, "You are witnesses, and so is God, how devoutly and uprightly and blamelessly we behaved toward you believers" (1 Thess. 2:10). He explained, "For we have regard for what is honorable, not only in the sight of the Lord, but also in the sight of men" (2 Cor. 8:21).

Paul knew the power of Christ to form integrity in and through every believer, calling us to "approve the things that are excellent, in order to be sincere and blameless until the day of Christ" (Phil. 1:10). He further urged believers to "prove yourselves to be blameless and innocent, children of God above reproach in the midst of a crooked and perverse generation, among whom you appear as lights in the world" (Phil. 2:15). Peter, writing about our lifestyle before the Lord's return, states, "Therefore, beloved, since you look for these things, be diligent to be found by Him in peace, spotless and blameless" (2 Peter 3:14).

The gospel defines and delivers empowerment for integrity. We know that those who lead the church are required to be "above reproach"—examples of holistic integrity before the ones they lead (1 Tim. 3:1–13; Titus 1:1–9). In a real sense, Christ does not call you to a standard of integrity. He is the standard of integrity and will live through you to demonstrate His character to a dark world.

The Tests and Testimony of a Life of Integrity

In Psalm 26, likely written around the same time as Psalm 15, David prayed, "Vindicate me, O Lord, for I have walked in my integrity."[9] David knew the blessing God had promised those who cling to integrity. Psalm 84 (also written on the same occasion, but on David's behalf by the sons of Korah)[10] declares, "For the Lord God is a sun and shield. The Lord gives grace and glory; He does not withhold the good from those who live with integrity. Happy is the person who trusts in You, Lord of Hosts!" (vv. 11–12 HCSB).

Late in life, as he led God's people in worship at the dedication of the temple, David prayed, "Since I know, O my God, that You try the heart and delight in uprightness, I, in the integrity of my heart, have willingly offered all these things; so now with joy I have seen Your people, who are present here, make their offerings willingly to You" (1 Chron. 29:17).

David's youngest son, Solomon, having witnessed the trials and triumphs of his father, would eventually articulate the blessings of integrity. Maybe he had Dad in mind when he wrote them. Perhaps he reflected on the recklessness of his older brother Absalom.

- "He who walks in integrity walks securely, but he who perverts his ways will be found out." (Prov. 10:9)
- "The integrity of the upright will guide them, but the crookedness of the treacherous will destroy them." (Prov. 11:3)
- "Better is a poor man who walks in his integrity than he who is perverse in speech and is a fool." (Prov. 19:1)
- "A righteous man who walks in his integrity—how blessed are his sons after him." (Prov. 20:7)

Yes, security, guidance, blessing, and a godly heritage. These became the enduring testimony of David's Psalm 15 moment and thus memorialized in a song that millions have cherished ever since.

The big bad wolf of pragmatism, hypocrisy, compartmentalization—and various winds of compromise—still roars. Build with the integrity of biblical brick. You'll never regret it.

Never Shaken Application

- If your life right now was actually a house built with bricks, what top five key "integrity ingredients" do you hope will compose those bricks? Why are these most significant for you?
- Think of the three most important people in your life. How do you want to demonstrate integrity to each of them? What influence do you hope this will ultimately have in their lives? Ask the Lord to more fully shape this characteristic in your life, according to the truths in this chapter.

- Review the verses from Proverbs cited at the end of the chapter. Based on these truths, try to summarize why integrity is important to you.

Chapter 4

THE REASSURANCE
OF RIGHT LIVING

*He who walks with integrity, and **works righteousness**,*
And speaks truth in his heart.

PSALM 15:2

If I try to hold this psalm up as a mirror,
I see not my own face, but the face of my saviour.
Only he can ascend that "holy hill"
and I will have to ascend with him or not at all.

MALCOLM GUITE

At the age of forty-two, my unchurched mother met a pastor's wife. My mom was trying to recruit her as a customer for a cosmetics business. The church lady eventually persuaded my mom to follow Christ, leading her to a dramatic conversion. I don't remember the transformation. I was only one year old and oblivious to spiritual things (actually, most things). Her decision to follow Jesus was first in our family, but my dad and two older brothers trusted Christ soon after.

Growing up, I was raised in a spiritual hothouse. My parents probably hung out more at the old Baptist church than did the pastor. On any given week, they were following up on newcomers, leading people to Jesus, organizing the church kitchen, ushering, and singing in the choir. He who is forgiven much loves much.

When my dad died in 2005, five years after my mom, my older brothers (eleven and fifteen years my senior) started sharing stories. Crazy stories. Stories I never knew. Jim and Dennis were both raised in a "before Christ" environment. I learned that, before salvation, my mom had been married five times. My biological dad was husband number three and five. Their lives were marked by violent fights, affairs, dysfunction, and much unhappiness. My dad's promising Air Force career had been truncated by his domestic difficulties and struggles with alcohol.

On several occasions, I asked my parents about their pre-salvation life. They never provided the juicy details as dramatized by the tales from my brothers. They simply noted that in matters of faith, they previously believed that when they got to heaven, God would weigh the good things done against the bad things, and maybe they would be good enough—perhaps lucky enough—to make it through the "pearly gates." Obviously, that approach would not have worked for them. It never works for anyone. The Bible makes that clear. "There is none righteous, not even one" (Rom. 3:10), and "all have sinned and fall short of the glory of God" (Rom. 3:23).

Yet in Psalm 15, David sings a reflective tune declaring that a true worshiper who really knows God intimately is one who "works righteousness." So, how is that possible? By that standard, who can make the grade? Before we unpack the truth of Yahweh's righteousness and sink the roots of our confidence deeply into the righteousness we have in Jesus, let's review.

The Blessing of Doing Right

Draw that straight line again from this early truth in Psalm 15 to the end. The first stanza of the song speaks of the need to be a person who "does what is right" (v. 2 ESV). The culminating line promises that this individual will "never be shaken" (v. 5). Who would not want to embrace that good promise?

David had been wronged. That's why he is where he is. Defamed and deserted. Broken and banished. That's a challenging moment to choose the right thing for the right reason. But it is the crucial moment to do so.

We've all been there. Pain and perplexity can baffle our senses and weaken our will to choose rightly. When we are betrayed, our flesh wants to engage in a battle of argument and anger. When we've been hurt, we want revenge. David's humanity was again in the crucible of some big decisions.

Scholars believe that Psalm 143 is another psalm David sang while exiled by Absalom.[1] David cried out, "Hear my prayer, O Lord, give ear to my supplications! Answer me in Your faithfulness, in Your righteousness! And do not enter into judgment with Your servant, for in Your sight no man living is righteous." He had been judged by the illegitimate court of fickle political allegiances. He does not want the judgment of almighty God upon the reactions that war in his soul.

So David says, "No man living is righteous" (143:2). But to experience God, he must be one who "works righteousness" (15:2). He is wisely crying out for righteousness, not his own. He knows the evil potential lurking in his grief-stricken heart. He is saddled with hard choices. Inspired by the wisdom of the Spirit, David says, "Answer me . . . in Your righteousness" (143:1).

Now we are onto something. Something that a moral mess-up like me can trust. Something an unsettled soul will want to fully embrace to experience this never-shaken life.

The Downside of the Wrong Choice

The flip side of that behavioral coin is one all too familiar—and packed with fallout. It's a very precarious existence when you do what is *not* right. You torment your conscience. Important relationships are broken. Innocent people get hurt. You get fired. You damage your future. You go to jail. Maybe you die. At best, you are miserable (or at least you should be).

David certainly had not always embraced what was right. He had also been the recipient of wrong treatment from others. For years he was an unjustly accused fugitive because Saul was bent on what was not right. At the moment, David has been banished by a son who clearly has done things that are wrong and conniving. But now, through his songs of lonely, longing reflection, he sets his heart again toward integrity built with the solid bricks of what is righteous. (The rest of Psalm 15 gets even more specific as to what that looks like for him—and for us.)

A Short Refresher on Righteousness

The notion of righteousness appears in the Bible over five hundred times—139 times in the Psalms. Clearly, it is a significant theme. As it is used in Psalm 15:2, it means to meet a standard and to be firm. God has always blessed His people with His righteousness—by faith, not by human works.

The first reference to righteousness in the Bible was the account of Abraham. God promised him countless future generations, although his wife Sarah had been barren and they were both old. Genesis 15:6 states, "He believed in the LORD; and He reckoned it to him as righteousness." This was not about Abraham's human ability to do good, although he was a godly man. Instead, God deemed him righteous because of his absolute faith in God's character and promise. One commentator notes, "Abram entrusted his future to what God would do for him as opposed to what he could do for himself to obtain the promises."[2]

In God's eternal plan, the basis for any person being declared righteous, Abraham included, was the perfect sacrifice of Jesus Christ. Faith has always been the means of that righteousness, even if it was looking forward to a yet-to-be-revealed Messiah. So, our assurance of an unshakable life is faith in what Jesus accomplished on our behalf. We trust all He now promises to us because of His finished work. Romans 3:22 describes it as "the righteousness of God through faith in Jesus Christ for all those who believe."

Romans 4:5–6 assures us, "But to the one who does not work, but believes in Him who justifies the ungodly, his faith is credited as righteousness, just as David also speaks of the blessing on the man to whom God credits righteousness apart from works." Our works will never make us righteous. David knew this too. He relied on God's mercy for his righteousness. "How blessed is he whose transgression is forgiven, whose sin is covered! How blessed is the man to whom the LORD does not impute iniquity, and in whose spirit there is no deceit!" (Ps. 32:1–2).

I remember training people in our church to be effective in personal evangelism. To illustrate the futility of trusting our works to save us from God's holy condemnation of our sin, we used the analogy of an omelet made of some good eggs and some rotten ones. Three good eggs and three rotten eggs make for a lousy omelet. Even five good eggs and one rotten one—still a bad omelet. Our sin-infected efforts to be and do better cannot make us right before a holy God, even if our good works outbalance our bad ones, as my parents had hoped. Walter Henrichsen clarified:

> If people went to heaven by their own righteousness, it would be unfair in that it would require what not all have: knowledge, wealth, works, morality, etc. If you went to heaven by your works and died early, you would miss your chance to perform. If access to heaven were by your morality, and you were raised in a depraved environment, you would be handicapped. God, in His infinite grace, makes heaven available on the basis of what He did, not your own accomplishments.[3]

The work of Christ is the divine solution for making sinful people right with a holy God. "He made Him who knew no sin to be sin on our behalf, so that we might become the righteousness of God in Him" (2 Cor. 5:21). The significant theological word to describe this is "imputation." In simplest terms, this means that God counted our sin against Christ so that He would pay the penalty of that sin on our behalf. He also credits Christ's righteousness to us, declaring that we are now right with God through faith in Jesus. We are now righteous in our standing with God. The Westminster Shorter Catechism summarizes it by saying that God "accepts us as righteous in his sight, only for the righteousness of Christ *imputed to us*, and received by faith alone."[4]

Charles Spurgeon's reassuring words underscore this truth: "Saints are so righteous in Jesus Christ that they are more righteous than Adam was before he fell, for he had but a creature righteousness, and they have the righteousness of the Creator. He had a righteousness which he lost, but believers have a righteousness which they can never lose, an everlasting righteousness."[5]

Doing What We Are

We know what God now promises about our standing. Our new identity as Christians is "righteous." We are called to walk according to who we really are—by doing righteously. This only happens by the same grace and faith that has made us right to start with. "But the righteous man shall live by faith" (Rom. 1:17). This faith is our daily key to right living. First Peter 2:24 affirms, "He Himself bore our sins in His body on the cross, so that we might die to sin and live to righteousness." I love the way one writer captured it: "Righteousness is choosing to have faith in Christ to give us the strength to do the right thing even when it's difficult."[6]

God's grace has made it so. Christ in us continues to make it so. Titus 2:11–12 offers profound encouragement: "For the grace of

God has appeared, bringing salvation to all men, instructing us to deny ungodliness and worldly desires and to live sensibly, righteously and godly in the present age." The grace of Jesus instructs us to live righteously—even in this ungodly and unsettled age. We could say that without Christ, people are doing in order to be. Christians are being in order to do.

Psalm 15 ultimately points us to Christ and the character He can produce in His people. The resurrected Christ encountered two disciples walking on a road to a town called Emmaus. As He taught them about Himself, He explained, "These are My words which I spoke to you while I was still with you, that all things which are written about Me in the Law of Moses and the Prophets and the Psalms must be fulfilled" (Luke 24:44). His life was the fulfillment of so many of the prophecies and truths found in the Psalms—including the character qualities of a Psalm 15 disciple.

> **WITHOUT CHRIST, PEOPLE ARE DOING IN ORDER TO BE. CHRISTIANS ARE BEING IN ORDER TO DO.**

As Dane Ortlund has noted, "It is not a question, then, of whether *Christ* is the one who does Psalm 15, or whether *we* are; the answer is both, and in that order."[7]

The Power to Choose What Is Right

We do not hope to come into God's presence based on our righteous deeds. Instead, we are righteous because His presence has come into us. Our life is found entirely in Him. First Corinthians 1:30 affirms, "But by His doing you are in Christ Jesus, who became to us wisdom from God, and righteousness and sanctification, and redemption." Jesus is our righteousness. We have that "holy hill" presence indwelling us through the Holy Spirit. We can now live by His personal power every day.

WE DO NOT HOPE TO COME INTO GOD'S PRESENCE BASED ON OUR RIGHTEOUS DEEDS. INSTEAD, WE ARE RIGHTEOUS BECAUSE HIS PRESENCE HAS COME INTO US.

David knew the presence of the Holy Spirit. In his great prayer of confession, he cried, "Do not take Your Holy Spirit from me" (Ps. 51:11). As the Spirit inspired David with the song of Psalm 15, I believe He would also work in David to accomplish all it entailed. Old Testament saints did not have the assurance of the permanent, personal indwelling of the Spirit as we do. Instead, the Spirit would come upon and indwell certain individuals for the assignment He had given them. Such was the case with David. He knew—and desperately needed—the power of the Holy Spirit. How much more should you and I depend on the indwelling Spirit to empower us to live righteously?

Spirit-Prompted Righteous Desire

I love the truth of Philippians 2:13: "For it is God who is at work in you, both to will and to work for His good pleasure." The New Living Translation reads, "For God is working in you, giving you the desire and the power to do what pleases him." Without desire, there is no determination to do the right thing. So, we must ask the Holy Spirit in us to give us a supernatural longing to live righteously. We then trust Him to work in and through us to walk accordingly. Jesus promised, "Blessed are those who hunger and thirst for righteousness, for they shall be satisfied" (Matt. 5:6).

Spirit-Guided Righteous Decisions

Our spiritual health and present character are the product of our regular choices. To do the right thing, we must choose to rely on the Spirit to lead us in all ways wise and righteous. Galatians 5:16 compels us to "walk by the Spirit, and you will not carry out the desire of the flesh." Our internal, personal, divine GPS guides us into all truth, directing us to walk in the ways of Jesus and for His glory (John 16:14, 33).

Spirit-Empowered Righteous Discipline

In our resolve to live righteously, the Holy Spirit imparts to us the essential character quality of self-discipline. "But the fruit of the Spirit is . . . self-control" (Gal. 5:22–23). He empowers us to regulate our conduct by principle—not emotion, convenience, or outside pressure. We've often heard, "No pain, no gain." If we do not embrace the immediate pain of discipline, we will eventually experience the lingering pain of disappointment and regret. Second Timothy 1:7 assures us, "For God has not given us a spirit of timidity, but of power and love and discipline."

I have often described the Christian life as an upstream swim in a downstream world. The current is swift. The water is infested with the temptations of compromise, fleshly reactions, and blatant disobedience. Our two "arm strokes" for righteous living are prayer and the Word. If we stop stroking, we get carried downriver.

> THE FLUSTERING CURRENTS OF A HARSH AND HARD-PRESSING WORLD WILL SURGE AGAINST YOU, PUSHING YOU TO COMPROMISE YOUR INTEGRITY.

As we swim forward, we must breathe—steadily. This breath is the life of the Spirit in us. Does the stroking stimulate the work of the Spirit? Or does the energy of the Spirit fuel the stroking? Yes!

Wise swimmers match their vigorous arm movement with a continual kick. Perhaps this would be the relational connection we need to overcome the backward-pushing influences. The right leg of fellowship. The left leg of service.

Count on it. The flustering currents of a harsh and hard-pressing world will surge against you, pushing you to compromise your integrity. They will seduce you toward the wrong choices. Swirls of sin and eddies of enticement will attempt to turn you sideways. So, whatever you do, don't try to be good by your feeble resolve to do the right thing. Left to yourself, like my unsaved parents, the bad will win out and weigh you down, thereby leaving you heartless and hopeless.

Keep stroking. Keep kicking. Keep breathing. Swim onward to Jesus. He is your righteousness. He lives in you to provide real righteousness, especially when you are strangely unsettled.

Never Shaken Application

- In what way do you see people trying to be righteous through their religious works? Why is this not enough? If you can think of a specific person who is on this path, ask God for an opportunity to tell them about the gospel of grace and the life they can find through an authentic relationship with Jesus.
- Review Philippians 2:13. In what specific way do you sense the need for greater desire and power from Christ to do the right thing, even when it's difficult? What specific occasions come to mind as opportunities to trust Him for this grace?
- As you "swim upstream in a downstream world," what adjustments might you need to make in your daily or weekly routines in order to live righteously by Christ's indwelling power?

Chapter 5

THE EPICENTER OF AUTHENTICITY

He who walks with integrity, and works righteousness,
*And **speaks truth in his heart** . . .*

PSALM 15:2

We are so afraid of silence that we chase ourselves from one event to
the next in order not to have to spend a moment alone with
ourselves, in order not to have to look at ourselves in the mirror.

DIETRICH BONHOEFFER

It was a long and miserable year. The months passed slowly, like molasses in winter, after David's indiscretion with Bathsheba, the murder of her husband, and various attempts to cover it all up. God graciously gave David months to confess his sin. When he did not, the Lord sent the prophet Nathan to confront him. These were miserable months of inner turmoil. Reflecting later on the despair of his prolonged concealment, David wrote:

When I kept silent about my sin, my body wasted away through my groaning all day long. For day and night Your hand was heavy upon me; my vitality was drained away as with the fever heat of summer. (Ps. 32:3–4)

One writer describes it well:

David wasn't relaxing and taking life easy, sipping lemonade on his patio, during the aftermath of his adultery. Count on it . . . he had sleepless nights. He could see his sin written across the ceiling of his room as he tossed and turned in bed. He saw it written across the walls. He saw it on the plate where he tried to choke down his meals. He saw it on the faces of his counselors. He was a miserable husband, an irritable father, a poor leader, and a songless composer. He lived a lie but he couldn't escape the truth.[1]

That was until the prophet's confrontation cut David to the core. In deep repentance, the guilty king penned Psalm 51. He came to an earnest and honest confession of his sin before God. It seems the tipping point of his spiritual restoration was the realization, "Behold, You desire truth in the innermost being, and in the hidden part You will make me know wisdom" (Ps. 51:6).

Truth in the heart. The fuel of righteousness. The core material for a house of integrity. The glue for a life where all the pieces fit together. The pathway to restored joy.

How blessed is he whose transgression is forgiven, whose sin is covered! How blessed is the man to whom the LORD does not impute iniquity, and in whose spirit there is no deceit! . . . I acknowledged my sin to You, and my iniquity I did not hide; I said, "I will confess my transgressions to the LORD"; and You forgave the guilt of my sin. (Ps. 32:1, 2, 5)

David admitted his duplicity. He resolved to cherish truth in the inmost part. He was freed from the burden of pretense. He rejoiced in the blessing of purity. He soared from sullen misery to a shout of joy. He asked God for restored gladness in Psalm 51, "Make me to hear joy and gladness, let the bones which You have broken rejoice" (v. 8). He savored it after his confession in Psalm 32, "Be glad in the LORD and rejoice, you righteous ones; and shout for joy, all you who are upright in heart" (v. 11). He once again embraced the promise of an unshaken life.

The truth that "man looks at the outward appearance, but the LORD looks at the heart" had reawakened in David (1 Sam. 16:7). This was why God chose David. It was a matter of the heart. This was the ongoing basis on which the Almighty would bless David.

God is never done with His heart surgery and soul-strengthening until we have new hearts in eternity. John Owen wrote, "God comes to us with a gauge that can go right to the bottom. His instrument of trial digs deep into the depths and innermost part of the soul. It allows man to see clearly what is truly in him, and what type of metal he is made of."[2] In the meantime, and in every moment, we must embrace the Lord's command, "Watch over your heart with all diligence, for from it flow the springs of life" (Prov. 4:23).

> **THE MOST DANGEROUS LIES WE TELL ARE THE ONES WE TELL OURSELVES ABOUT OURSELVES.**

Consequential Heart Conversations

The most dangerous lies we tell are the ones we tell ourselves about ourselves. Internal deception is an everyday possibility. Psalm 15 calls us to reject the lies we embrace in the soul's recesses. Truth in the heart is the epicenter of authenticity.

Psalm 15:2 isolates the internal reasonings of the mind. They occur within us all day, every day. Even now, you are responding to the words on this page with some self-conversation. You've probably been talking to yourself while reading this book. "How many pages are in this chapter?" "I'm not sure I agree with that." "My husband needs to read this one!" "I need to underline and remember that thought." "Ouch. That hurt!"

We have internal conversations and reasonings all the time. "For as he thinks within himself, so he is" (Prov. 23:7).

The heart is paramount in Scripture. The New International Version (NIV) references the heart 546 times! But the heart is more than the four-chamber, blood-pumping station residing in your chest. It is mission control for our emotions, thoughts, and will. It is often synonymous with our character, decisions, and commitments.

Writers John Trent and Rick Hicks summarize the heart's importance:

- It is the source of speech (see Luke 6:45)
- It is the source of thoughts (see Matt. 15:19)
- It is the source of actions (see Matt. 15:19)
- It remembers (see Luke 2:51)
- It understands (see Matt. 13:15)
- It decides (see 2 Cor. 9:7)
- It is the source of emotions (see Acts 2:26)
- It believes God (see Rom. 10:9–10)
- It loves (see Mark 12:30, 33)
- It is known by God (see Acts 1:24)[3]

The medical field knows the vital importance of a heart monitor when addressing cardiac illness or weakness. Psalm 15 calls us to submit to the accuracy and power of solid truth to monitor our core in a world that assaults the essential vitality of a good and honest heart.

Choosing the Core Truth

I can only imagine the allure of the lies that might have been attacking David's innermost being in a devastating moment like this.

- There's no hope.
- Poor little old me. I am such a victim.
- I'm going to fix all of this. I have the power and experience to do it.
- These traitors! They are the problem, and I'm going to give them their due.
- That Absalom! I'll get my revenge.
- Maybe I should end it all.

Perhaps God's message of truth to David in this moment was something like, "My son—this is the time to tell yourself the truth about yourself once again. Take care of your heart. Learn from me in this teachable moment. Let me transform you as I have done before. I desire truth in the innermost being, and in the hidden part, I will impart true wisdom. I can show you the way forward. You will come forth as gold."

Do *you* hear His still, small voice right now? As your marriage is coming apart at the seams? As your job is sucking the life out of you? As friends turn against you? As you are coddling some secret sin? As the daily news is driving you mad? As you feel such anger toward politicians? When your kids seem hell-bent on rebellion? As you navigate anxiety about the future of your family? As you are worried about your finances?

I cannot help but wonder what truth captured David's heart as he paused his song, set aside his quill, and deliberated the moment. Maybe his thoughts emerged with helpful clarity and unswerving conviction:

- God is sovereign, and I can trust Him, even now.
- It's not my kingdom; it's God's.
- Vengeance is the Lord's, not mine.
- I am still living with the consequences of my previous sins, but God is a gracious restorer.

- The Lord has my life in His hands.
- I must deal with myself and trust God to deal with others.
- I must set my heart on Him, not my circumstances.

In the good, the bad, and the ugly of everyday life we must choose what we are going to believe. Psalm 15 calls us to choose what is true at the core of our soul.

The Musing of the Saints

The New Testament offers numerous warnings about the danger of self-deception. We find a practical call to speak the truth in our hearts.

When you think you are absolutely "right," feel superior in your effort to win an argument, or are convinced you have it all figured out, speak truth in your heart.

Let no man deceive himself. If any man among you thinks
that he is wise in this age, he must become foolish, so that he
may become wise. (1 Cor. 3:18)

When you believe that you'll never get caught or that your present ungodly behaviors will not have consequences for you or others, speak the truth in your heart. Conversely, when you think your sincere spiritual efforts do not matter or that the Lord will not reward your faithfulness—speak the truth in your heart.

Do not be deceived, God is not mocked; for whatever a man
sows, this he will also reap. (Gal. 6:7)

When you are satisfied with simply hearing or reading the truth but not experiencing fundamental transformation, or when you think Sunday sermons are for others more than they are for you, speak the truth in your heart.

But prove yourselves doers of the word, and not merely hearers *who delude themselves.* (James 1:22)

When you are satisfied or even sanctimonious about your religious behavior but tolerate a lack of godly discipline in your speech, relationships, thoughts, and behaviors—speak the truth in your heart.

If anyone thinks himself to be religious, and yet does not bridle his tongue but *deceives his own heart*, this man's religion is worthless. (James 1:26)

When the Holy Spirit convicts you about any sin, whether it seems small or significant, don't justify or pretend it's not so bad—speak the truth in your heart.

If we say that we have no sin, we are *deceiving ourselves* and the truth is not in us. (1 John 1:8)

When you have isolated yourself from others and have distanced your heart from the encouragement, loving confrontation, or helpful input from family or friends—speak the truth in your heart.

But encourage one another day after day, as long as it is still called "Today," so that none of you will be hardened by *the deceitfulness of sin.* (Heb. 3:13)

Step One Toward Truthful Recovery

The 12-step program of Alcoholics Anonymous has recognized this powerful principle. Self-honesty is step one. You can't attend an AA meeting declaring, "Hi, my name is Bill, and I have alcohol in my home every once in a while." Nope. "Hey, I'm Susan, and my mother was a habitual alcoholic, and, you know, I've struggled with it off and on." Nada. "Howdy, I'm Charlie, and my wife thinks I need to be here, but I'm not sure." Try again. The only acceptable opening line is: "Hi, I'm Laura, and I am an alcoholic."

For the Christ follower, it might sound like, "Good morning, Father, I am Your child, and I am . . . [truthful self-honesty]" or "Dear God, You know what just happened, and I need to . . . [truthful self-honesty]" or maybe, "Lord, it's been a rough day, and I admit that I . . . [truthful self-honesty]." Or "Lord, I am discouraged, but I know your Word promises that . . . [truthful self-honesty]."

Dangerous Defaults

Our explanations, excuses, and exaggerations often show a common tendency to compromise truth. We've all done it. We describe what we did or offer "our take" on what happened, knowing in our heart that it is not actually true. Like the guy who came home from a fishing trip and didn't catch anything. He stopped in the meat market and said, "I want to buy that big trout, but I want you to throw it to me over the counter so I can tell my buddies I caught this fish." A legal testimony is supposed to be "the truth, the whole truth, and nothing but the truth." More importantly, a biblical explanation should be the same.

I heard years ago that "an excuse is simply a lie wrapped in a reason." We make excuses to deny responsibility and avoid the consequences of our mistakes. We don't want to look as flawed as we really are. I remember hearing an audio series by a psychologist who interviewed hundreds of inmates. He estimated that over 95 percent of those he interviewed had some excuse as to why it was not their fault that they were in prison. Excuses like, "The devil made me do it." Some offered elaborate stories of why it was some other guy's fault or "It was my mother. She fed me oatmeal and warped my sense of reality." These lies left little hope for real reform.

Beyond our common excuses, we can also tend to exaggerate.

Through exaggeration, we stretch the truth. We try to make ourselves look better than we are. Exaggeration is evidence of an insecure soul with a greater desire to impress people than to please God. Wayne Grudem cuts to the chase:

> Each time a person speaks the truth or lies, he aligns himself either with God, "who never lies" (Titus 1:2), or with Satan, "a liar and the father of lies" (John 8:44).
>
> A person who tells the truth (or remains silent), even in a difficult situation, faithfully represents his Creator as one who tells the truth and does not lie, and therefore becomes more closely conformed to the image of God. In addition . . . telling the truth often requires inward trust in God to govern the circumstances and the outcome of the situation.[4]

On countless occasions I have needed Grudem's wisdom. An "inward trust in God" could have given me a deeper resolve to trust Him for the uncomfortable consequences of absolute truthfulness rather than leaning on my own subjective schemes. Schemes that weaken my integrity and undermine authentic relationships.

Heart Realities

It's not an encouraging reality—but it is reality. The Bible says that we have a catastrophic heart problem. Jeremiah 17:9–10 warns:

> "The heart is more deceitful than all else and is desperately sick; who can understand it? I, the LORD, search the heart, I test the mind, even to give to each man according to his ways, according to the results of his deeds."

Some key points resonate here. First, we cannot ultimately understand the dreadful potential of the heart to wreak havoc in our lives.

Second, only God ultimately knows the dark and deceptive recesses of the heart. Third, God evaluates us according to our heart—not just our words, wealth, accomplishments, or appearance. Finally, the heart produces the actual fruit of our deeds.

The context leading up to Jeremiah's pronouncement on the peculiarities of the human heart gives us more clarity and warning. In summary, God says, "Cursed is the man who trusts in mankind and makes flesh his strength, and whose heart turns away from the LORD" (Jer. 17:5). This person's existence will be like a dried-up shrub in a barren, salty desert—under the judgment of God.

Now the good news: "Blessed is the man who trusts in the LORD and whose trust is the LORD" (Jer. 17:7). This heart will be fearless, confident, fruitful, and anxiety-free.

Live No Lies

In unsettled times we must recognize and reaffirm that we cannot trust our hearts or rely on our own strength. Yet we have a sure anchor and a strong confidence in our quest for interior, gut-level truth—from which absolute security and strength flow.

We can invite God to search and test us. We must desire a profound work of the sufficient Word of God to expose lies and infuse truth. Here is our hope and expectation:

> For the word of God is living and active and sharper than
> any two-edged sword, and piercing as far as the division
> of soul and spirit, of both joints and marrow, and able to
> judge the thoughts and intentions of the heart. And there is
> no creature hidden from His sight, but all things are open
> and laid bare to the eyes of Him with whom we have to do.
> (Heb. 4:12–13)

The Bible is entirely sufficient to expose our questionable explanations, lame excuses, and flimsy exaggerations. The word brings reality to our very thoughts and intentions. No more shell games. Just the truth, the whole truth, and nothing but the truth. With the help of the all-knowing God.

We must also embrace prayerful reliance on the "Spirit of truth" who guides us into all truth (John 16:13). I love the fact that when we pray, we can open the Bible and have a conversation with the Author (the Holy Spirit), who lives in us, to help us clearly understand all that He meant by what He said. He then makes it real in our hearts to produce transformation through applying His truth, with the indwelling power to live it. Here is the daily pathway to "truth in the heart."

> WE CAN OPEN THE BIBLE AND HAVE A CONVERSATION WITH THE AUTHOR (THE HOLY SPIRIT) WHO LIVES IN US TO HELP US CLEARLY UNDERSTAND ALL THAT HE MEANT BY WHAT HE SAID.

Free Every Day

Jesus promised that those who would embrace His gospel "will know the truth, and the truth will make you free" (John 8:32). Certainly, this is our assurance in terms of our eternal salvation. We know that we can be free from the penalty and power of sin. Someday we'll be free from the presence of sin. But it is an ongoing promise for the Christ follower who continues to perceive and experience the truth in Jesus.

We can be free from the anxiety-inducing façade. Free from the fear of being found out. Free from false beliefs. Free from a guilty conscience. Free to do what is right even if it is costly. Free to trust the goodness and grace of God when the stakes of honesty are high. Free to live out the righteousness of Christ in us. Free to walk daily in authentic integrity. Free to ask the highest and best questions in the toughest of times. Free to experience God in an intimate, abiding relationship. Free to bear fruit for His glory.

An ancient writer said, "He who knows his sin is greater than he who makes someone rise from the dead. He who can really cry one hour about himself is greater than he who teaches the whole world and he who knows his own weaknesses is greater than he who sees the angels."[5] God has not called us to live a spectacular life, just a sincere one.

David had to relearn the lesson as he crafted his song through the fog of a devastating experience. The notes he sang surely stirred deeper obedience. His inspired lyrics formed the way forward. His faithful God brought clarity through the confusion.

Let this be your song. Embrace truth. Live righteously. Walk with integrity. Remain . . . never shaken.

Never Shaken Application

- Reflect on the internal conversations you've had with yourself over the last few days. What has the focus been? What has shaped that focus? What percentages have been fueled by emotion, circumstances, the opinions of people? Has the truth of God's Word been primary? If so, how?

- As you reflect on the tendency to compromise truth through explanations, exaggerations, and excuses, which of these seems to most commonly occur in your heart? How can you make a change to embrace a more biblical self-honesty?

- Tomorrow, as you read your Bible, make a more conscious effort to allow the indwelling Spirit to guide you into honest application and transformation. As you do so, how do you think it will specifically affect your attitudes and choices throughout the day?

Chapter 6

KEEPING YOUR LIPS FROM SINKING SHIPS

He does not slander with his tongue . . .

PSALM 15:3

An unbridled tongue is the chariot of the devil,
wherein he rides in triumph.

EDWARD REYNER

Years ago, I heard a humorous anecdote about how the Americans and Russians were at the height of the arms race during the Cold War years. They realized that if they continued, they might blow up the whole world. So one day, they sat down and decided to settle the entire dispute—with a dogfight. They would each have five years to breed the meanest and most vicious fighting canine in the world and match them against one another. Whoever won would rule the world. The defeated opponent would have to lay down their arms.

Naturally, the Russians worked hard. They found the biggest, most ferocious Doberman and Rottweiler females in the world and bred them with Siberian wolves. They selected only the strongest puppy from each litter. They fed them well and utilized steroids and trainers. Finally, after five years, they were convinced they had bred the winning canine. So no one would be harmed, they kept it in a cage with five-inch-thick steel.

When the day of the contest arrived, the Americans showed up with a strange contestant. It was a nine-foot-long dachshund. Naturally, everyone felt sorry for the Americans because they knew this was no match for this ferocious entrant of the Russians.

They opened the cages. The odd dachshund came waddling toward the Russian dog. The Russian dog snarled and bolted from the cage to charge the American entry. But when it got close enough to bite, the American contestant opened its mouth and consumed the Russian dog in one bite.

The Russians shook their heads in disbelief. They said, "We don't understand how this could've happened. We bred a dog that could devour any opponent." The Americans replied, "Well, that's nothing. We had our best plastic surgeons working for five years to make an alligator look like a dachshund."

You may know someone who has the appearance of the dachshund but the bite of an alligator. They may be a relative, friend, neighbor, church member, employee, employer, enemy, or even the person in the mirror.

Tales of the Tongue

Defamatory speech, disinformation campaigns, and disparaging declarations are now baked into our social culture like flour in a loaf of bread. Cable channel exposés, tell-all tabloids, reputation-ruining investigative reports, and derogatory tweets have become so common that we assume this is just how we should manage our day-to-day interactions.

Psalm 15 raises the bar on our common bantering and tells us that the God follower who lives in the security and strength of integrity "does not slander with his tongue" (v. 3).

The Hebrew word for slander means to "go about on foot." This describes the person who walks around whispering about others and spreading false or derogatory information. It is translated "backbiting" (NKJV). It happens when we pass on a tasty little tidbit about someone with the result of making them look bad—and in some cases, designed to make us look better by comparison.

Of course, no one needs to physically "walk about" anymore to unbridle some juicy slander. It can slip into conversation through the convenience of a smartphone. A quick text, a brief FaceTime, or an ill-motivated social media post will do the job. In today's internet-crazed environment where everyone can have a "platform" on countless outlets, the potential of unleashing unloving, even hateful, words is easier than ever. But just because I can say something derogatory about someone does not mean I should. In countless ways, slander is convenient. But God says it is still costly and cruel.

Serious Stuff

Contrary to modern-day acceptance, God hates slander (Prov. 6:16–19). He prohibits it among His people (Lev. 19:16). The ninth commandment forbids bearing false witness (Ex. 20:16). God declares that He will judge the slanderer (Ps. 101:5). Slander creates discord and destroys relationships (Prov. 11:9; 16:28; 17:9). We will give an account in eternity for every careless word, certainly including slander (Matt. 12:36). Christians who slander behave like the unsaved world (Titus 3:2). Paul says that slanderers have "an appearance of godliness" but have denied its power—and are to be avoided (2 Tim. 3:1–5 ESV). Paul even describes slander as the behavior of people who hate God (Rom. 1:30). James calls it demonic behavior (James 3:15–16).

The Greek word translated slander is *diabolos*, much akin to Satan, who accuses Christians day and night before God (Rev. 12:10). The New Testament term is also translated as speaking against, defaming, or blaspheming another person. It's integrated very closely with gossiping, tale-bearing, or backstabbing. The temptation toward slander is real and regular.

Years ago, someone on our staff shared a morning prayer that seemed appropriate.

Dear Lord, so far today I'm doing okay. I've not gossiped, I've not lost my temper, I've not been greedy, grumpy, nasty, selfish or over-indulgent. However, I'm going to get out of bed in a few minutes, and I'll need a lot more help after that.

Avoiding slander is easy until we engage with people. We don't execute slander in a vacuum. We don't just wake up one day and think, "I am going to go pick some poor random soul out of a crowd and slander her." Slander assumes some interpersonal connection. Slander is typically an inappropriate reaction to a stressed relationship or deep-seated disagreement. The heart coddles hurt, jealousy, envy, insecurity, and other interpersonal trouble. The tongue unleashes its toxin as a natural response.

But, even in the hardest of relationships, we need God's perspective and prescription for speech that honors Him and one another. Jon Bloom offers some helpful perspectives:

Slander occurs whenever someone says something untrue about someone else that results, intentionally or unintentionally, in damaging that someone else's reputation. And when it occurs, it becomes a divisive, discouraging, and confusing weight that often affects numerous people—sometimes many, many people.

Because of its poisonous power, it is one of the adversary's chief strategies to divide relationships and deter and derail the mission of the church. We must be on our guard against this closely clinging sin and frequently lay it aside.[1]

Restraint or Retaliation?

Earlier in David's reign, he was inspired to pen Psalm 101. This song established the ground rules for the worship of God in Israel. Psalm 101:5 says, "Whoever secretly slanders his neighbor, him I will destroy; no one who has a haughty look and an arrogant heart will I endure." David indeed remembered the seriousness of slander, even when his heart wanted to go there. He was exiled because he was smeared by a son, relatives, advisors, and loyal friends.

As David penned his Psalm 15 song, there were plenty of targets for potential slanderous discharge of his defense:

- Absalom, the self-consumed son, had betrayed and banished him.
- A half-crazed guy named Shimei publicly cursed David and threw stones as he escaped Jerusalem (2 Sam. 16:5–8).
- Ahithophel, the priest, one of David's trusted advisors, broke loyalty and even advised Absalom to publicly sleep with David's concubines to shame the exiled king (2 Sam. 16:20–22).
- A slew of other duped advisors and friends defected and joined the rebellion.
- At least twenty thousand soldiers joined Absalom's deadly pursuit of David (2 Sam. 18:6–8).

Lesser men would have unleashed a barrage of verbal bombs. But in this moment, God was teaching David again the essential truths of a life of absolute integrity. An unshaken life. The kind of speech and character we desperately need today.

We all have situations that make it hard to bridle our fired-up tongues. James empathized with our dilemma when he wrote, "For we all stumble in many ways. If anyone does not stumble in what he says, he is a perfect man, able to bridle the whole body as well" (James 3:2). Yet he elevated the divine expectation as he went on to explain:

> But no one can tame the tongue; it is a restless evil and full of deadly poison. With it we bless our Lord and Father, and with it we curse men, who have been made in the likeness of God; from the same mouth come both blessing and cursing. My brethren, these things ought not to be this way. Does a fountain send out from the same opening both fresh and bitter water? Can a fig tree, my brethren, produce olives, or a vine produce figs? Nor can salt water produce fresh. (James 3:8–12)

Proverbs 18:21 affirms, "The tongue can bring death or life; those who love to talk will reap the consequences" (NLT).

Guarding the Valuables

Speaking against another person is potentially a devastating relational incident. Proverbs 22:1 says, "A good name is to be more desired than great wealth, favor is better than silver and gold." A person's reputation is their most prized possession. So, rather than slandering them, I would be more kind to break into their house, ransack all their goods, steal all their jewelry, take all their heirlooms, empty all the funds in their bank account, hijack their IRAs, and abscond with their home title.

Their good name is more precious than all these things. When tempted to speak ill of another person in conversation or a social media post, we should consider the devastating impact that can result. Sure, they can pay some website to help them defend their online reputation. Still, your words may inflict aching and enduring pain. Proverbs 26:28 states, "A lying tongue hates those it crushes, and a flattering mouth works ruin."

Heart Problems = Tongue Problems

In Mark 7:20–23, Jesus asserts that slander proceeds from a defiled heart; it is not just a surface behavior. He also claims that our inner person is the source of evil speech because our mouth is simply the overflow of that which fills the heart (Luke 6:45).

So, what temptations could have been plaguing David's soul in this severe trial? What are our heart problems when our tongue becomes a tool of derision and division?

> **THE CRITIC WHO BEGINS WITH HIMSELF IS SOON TOO BUSY TO TAKE ON OUTSIDE CONTRACTS.**

First Peter 2:1 connects the dots clearly: "Therefore, putting aside all malice and all deceit and hypocrisy and envy and all slander." Notice again that slander is the outward action described in connection with internal attitudes—malice, deceit, hypocrisy, and envy.

Malice refers to ill will and spitefulness. Here's a troubled heart that seeks to harm.[2]

Deceit carries the idea of baiting for fish through stealth or treacherous means. Slander often involves the bending of the truth in subtle ways.

Hypocrisy (described in chapter 1 also) is rooted in the Greek idea of playing a part on the stage. Think pretense. Insincerity. Manipulation. Here's a self-deceived heart, usually with an overinflated view of oneself and a personal disdain or disrespect for others. It is akin to the person with a log in their eye, criticizing the speck in another's.

I heard it said many years ago, "There is so much that is bad about the best of us and good about the worst of us that it compels none of us to talk about the rest of us." I've learned that the critic who begins with himself is soon too busy to take on outside contracts.

Envy is jealousy over the good fortune of others. They have more or better than we have. So we compare ourselves and feel inferior or, conversely, insecure. There are two ways of making yourself appear better—either by your own merits or by taking advantage of the weaknesses of others. Slander often reveals more about our own internal sin than their shortcomings.

Here is practical wisdom: "Whoever belittles his neighbor lacks sense, but a man of understanding remains silent. Whoever goes about slandering reveals secrets, but he who is trustworthy in spirit keeps a thing covered" (Prov. 11:12–13 ESV). So, those loose lips that sink ships can reveal more about the talker than the target. He who slings mud, whether his intention or aim is accurate, is still left with muddy hands. Proverbs says the verbal attacker lacks sense and cannot be trusted.

Consider it a loan when you devastate someone with your slanderous words. Know that it will likely come back to you with interest. "He who digs a pit will fall into it, and he who rolls a stone, it will come back on him" (Prov. 26:27).

What to Do When Slandered

So, how should we respond when we are slandered or hurtfully demeaned? Ecclesiastes 7:21–22 offers a helpful perspective: "Also, do not take seriously all words which are spoken, so that you will not hear your servant cursing you. For you also have realized that you likewise have many times cursed others." Paraphrase: We all hurt others with our words. When you are the target, remember that you have been the propagator many times. Don't get overly offended or self-righteous about it. Proceed humbly.

Trust Your Reputation to God

The Bible promises that you will be persecuted if you endeavor to live a godly life in this fallen world (2 Tim. 3:12). Often, the persecution of the godly comes through a verbal attack. The lifelong testimony of David's life, reflected in the Psalms, reminds us that we often need to cry out to God in earnest trust and humble surrender when unfairly slandered. We find this common theme in David's songs (Pss. 31:13; 35:21; 41:5; 52:2; 55:21; 64:3; 109:2; 120:2; 140:3). Veteran pastor Ray Ortlund stated, "When (not if) your reputation suffers an undeserved injury, your quiet integrity over time will say all that needs to be said."[3] Here's a good reminder of what we should understand and how we should respond:

> The righteous is delivered from trouble, and the wicked walks into it instead. With his mouth the godless man would destroy his neighbor, but by knowledge the righteous are delivered. . . . Whoever belittles his neighbor lacks sense, but a man of understanding remains silent. (Prov. 11:8–9, 12 ESV)

The quiet integrity of knowledge and understanding can definitely bridle our questionable emotional reactions. We can cling, hard as it may be, to the truth that the Lord is our protection and the defender of our reputation. We know that the real scoreboard is not about the superficial arguments we win and counterattacks we can muster. The eternal scoreboard is in heaven. Our Divine Scorekeeper sees all and knows all. He never misses a call. We can trust that He is righteous and just. His vindication and reward are forever. We can lean on God in the fleeting moments when we are maligned or misunderstood.

Clarify and Confront

There are times when we must lovingly confront a fellow believer whose tongue is sinning in destructive ways against us or someone else. The Bible explains how we do this (Matt. 18:15–17). In summary, go to the person privately, clearly explaining the violation and impact of their words. If they repent, you have helped them and restored the relationship. If not, the process continues by inviting one or two others to verify the error. Again, the goal is repentance and restoration. The issue should go to the church's leaders if they are still immovable. Hopefully, the care shown in the process and the realization of the seriousness of the sin will bring this individual to the point of admitting their error and clearing their conscience. Otherwise, there is some doubt about the genuineness of their faith. In each church, the leadership should have biblical wisdom and courage in these conclusions.

See the Opportunity

Slanderous attacks from the unbelieving world give us a different opportunity. The model of Jesus is our ultimate aim: "And while being reviled, He did not revile in return; while suffering, He uttered no threats, but kept entrusting Himself to Him who judges righteously" (1 Peter 2:23).

Jesus commanded a peculiar but powerful response for the slandered.

> "Blessed are you when people insult you and persecute you, and falsely say all kinds of evil against you because of Me. Rejoice and be glad, for your reward in heaven is great; for in the same way they persecuted the prophets who were before you." (Matt. 5:11–12)

John Piper admits, "I would argue that this is the most difficult command in the Bible—namely, for Jesus's sake to feel joy and gladness when you are reviled and persecuted and slandered."[4] Yet, God gives supernatural grace to trust instead of tangling in a word war. He empowers us to live above the detractor's words by the consistency of the Spirit's fruit revealed to others through us.

Peter, writing to persecuted and slandered believers, challenged them to live submissive and respectful lives even in the toughest of times. He pointed to this God-honoring outcome: "For such is the will of God that by doing right you may silence the ignorance of foolish men" (1 Peter 2:15).

Here is our confidence and conviction when slander is taking its toll on our soul and reputation. God will deliver us. Our confidence is in our knowledge of Christ, truth, and wisdom. Our silence is more powerful than our bantering self-defense.

Learn and Grow

We also need to realize that some verbal attacks contain nuggets of needed truth about ourselves—truth we need to acknowledge humbly. The adage holds, "If one man calls you a donkey, ignore him. If two or more call you a donkey, get a saddle." So, we can even learn some things when hurtful words bring a helpful mirror, leading to humble acceptance and trust for the grace to keep growing.

So here is the solid ground for an unshaken life:

1. Acknowledge slander for what it is—a destructive sin that reflects a troubled heart.
2. Invite Scripture, the Holy Spirit, and an honest friend to help you evaluate your heart motivations of a loose tongue—including the attitudes that are sinful.
3. Repent and ask the Lord to examine and change your heart. Invite Him to empower you to exhibit the fruit of the Spirit in all expressions of your speech. Here is what that can look like: "Love, joy, peace, patience, kindness, goodness, faithfulness, gentleness, self-control" (Gal. 5:22–23). Life-giving words for sure. Titus affirmed this: "Malign no one . . . be peaceable, gentle, showing every consideration for all men" (Titus 3:2).
4. Respond humbly and biblically to slander when you are the recipient (review the points above).
5. Live a "never-shaken" life by knowing that your words are life-giving, your reputation belongs to God, and your testimony will declare the reality of a mighty Savior living and speaking through you.

Never Shaken Application

- In what ways has your tongue caused some relational pain in the past? What motivated that incident or pattern? What attitudes can you surrender to the Lord if that temptation arises again?
- Can you think of a time when you have been slandered? How did it affect you? Learning from that experience and the truth in this chapter, how might you respond differently in the future?
- Think of a relationship that could easily be threatened by unkind words. How can you be more intentional to speak life-giving words instead? What specific words do you hope to share in order to minister more graciously in this situation?

Chapter 7

DEFYING EVIL, DOING GOOD

He does not slander with his tongue,
***Nor does evil to his neighbor** . . .*

PSALM 15:3

Solving the reaction problem resolves more than half of our Christian life. People act; we react. They say something; we react. They show some kind of attitude; we react. We are simply full of reactions. Since the greater part of our life is composed of reactions, for us to react in the Christian way is acceptable to God.

WATCHMAN NEE

Earl (not his real name) planted himself tenaciously behind the single microphone placed at the front of a crowded church auditorium. Many months of careful calculation had preceded his pronouncements. In many ways, he was the ringleader for a small group of disgruntled long-term church members. They had conspired together and brought dozens of allegations against the elders, finance team, staff, and the new young pastor. After some earnest but failed attempts to resolve their mostly petty concerns, the elders enlisted a mediation team. At the recommendation of that team, it all culminated at this moment. The congregation gathered to hear all the behind-the-scenes drama. A vote of confidence for the leadership was announced to occur the following Sunday.

I was the new young pastor. I knew Earl well. I was keenly aware

87

of some significant issues in his life and family. I could see through the triviality and hypocrisy of his angst.

I sat in the front row, champing at the bit as Earl proceeded with his accusations. I knew that in thirty seconds or less, I could borrow the mic and completely discredit and humiliate the man. Sensing my seething temptation, my board chairman put his hand on mine as if to say, "Not now. Don't react." So, glued grudgingly in my seat, I endured his extended diatribe.

When the ordeal ended, I had avoided a mean-spirited spitting contest. I was grateful for the wisdom of an elder and the conviction of the Spirit that helped me embrace meekness over meanness. The vote of confidence was overwhelmingly supportive of the church leadership. Earl and his squad left the church, and the congregation was ready to move on to focus on our actual mission.

Like an overfilled water balloon waiting for the slightest prick before bursting, sometimes the pressure and conflicts of life can leave us on edge—ready to erupt in nasty reactions and deplorable behavior. It can happen to the best of us. We eventually regret that it prompted such a dreadful display of the worst of us.

Psalm 15:3 defines another character marker of the true God follower, one who will never be shaken. He refuses to do "evil to his neighbor." Our bent toward this "evil" might involve a long-calculated determination to enact a malicious payback plan. More often, it is an in-the-moment snap of odious emotion. Either way, Psalm 15:3 provides a line of conduct that the integrity-focused believer will not cross, tempting as it may be.

Hitting Close to Home

In this verse, "evil" refers to the intent to "muddy, pollute, or destroy another person's life, family, or business."[1] It carries the idea of inflicting misery or distress. The concern of this passage is not some random act of viciousness inflicted on the person who cut us off in traffic (although we've been tempted in those moments). This verse refers to evil inflicted on someone in a close relationship—probably not with an instrument of death but with the intention of some kind of pain.

A "neighbor" is not just that guy residing across the alley who infuriates us with his unruly barking dogs. Instead, this neighbor is someone in close relational proximity. Someone we know well. Someone we interact with regularly.

You've probably heard that most interpersonal violence occurs within a circle of family or friends. They are not random acts of evil but relational acts of evil. One particular report by the Bureau of Justice Statistics conveyed that 16 percent of murder victims were members of the defendant's family. Another 64 percent were murdered by friends or acquaintances. Only 20 percent were taken out by strangers.[2] So, the great temptation of the human soul is to nurture ill will, coddle negative emotions, and play out hurtful behaviors. We might do "evil" in the heat of the moment or deliberately over a span of time to someone we know.

Right now, you might recall a severe reaction unleashed on your spouse when they irritated you for the hundredth time. You remember the anger released on the rude child you raised. You might recall the effort to undermine the credibility of that work associate who was pursuing the same promotion as you. These actions are reactions—reactions to hurt, threats, or just plain irritation.

Watchman Nee noted, "At least half, if not more, of our lives are lived in reactions. . . . By observing how a person reacts, we can judge who he is. A Christian should not have unchristian reactions, nor can a non-Christian have true Christian reactions. If you want to know what sort of person someone is, just notice the kind of reactions he has."[3]

The Long Journey of Choices

In this present Psalm 15 moment, it would seem natural to give in to the anger that boils up after betrayal, abandonment, and shame. It would have been easy for David to seek revenge against his son Absalom. Instead, this chapter presents a decisive teaching moment for the reader in learning what it means to do good to enemies and leave vengeance in the hands of the Lord. We all face deep disappointments, rejection, and minor offenses. God offers wisdom and grace to remain unshaken.

Absalom's betrayal was not David's first lesson in the school of self-control and deep trust in the sovereign hand of an almighty God. David had already grappled with the heartache of being a recipient of the kind of evil that a jealous and mad "neighbor" can inflict. In

WE ALL FACE DEEP DISAPPOINTMENTS, REJECTION, AND MINOR OFFENSES. GOD OFFERS WISDOM AND GRACE TO REMAIN UNSHAKEN.

his early years, a spear-throwing king tried every tactic and trick in the book to make David disappear (1 Sam. 18:8–11). But David never "returned the favor" against his high-powered antagonist.

Saul violated God's anointing through personal disobedience (1 Sam. 15:1–35). In time, an evil spirit tormented him. Saul became the epitome of futile angst and fruitless aggression (1 Sam. 16:14; 18:10–12).

Putting aside a king's normal duties, Saul spent months chasing David through countless valleys, up and down scattered hillsides, and a variety of enemy territories. Eventually, he found David in a cave. Actually, David found *him* in a cave.

You may remember the story from 1 Samuel 24. It tells of a profound commitment to do good rather than evil toward a neighbor. Saul was pursuing David with three thousand soldiers when he went into a convenient cave to "relieve himself." Little did he know that David and his men, hiding in the recesses, had a front-row seat to this private moment. Despite the urging of his cohorts, David did not exact revenge on the sitting duck enemy-king. Instead, he quietly crept up and cut a corner of Saul's robe off while he was occupied with his business. David's rationale? "Far be it from me because of the LORD that I should do this thing to my lord, the LORD's anointed, to stretch out my hand against him, since he is the LORD's anointed" (1 Sam. 24:6).

After Saul left the cave and reunited with his troops, David cried out to Saul, announcing,

> "Behold, this day your eyes have seen that the LORD had given you today into my hand in the cave, and some said to kill you, but my eye had pity on you . . . know and perceive that there is no evil or rebellion in my hands, and I have not sinned against you, though you are lying in wait for my life to take it. . . . The LORD therefore be judge and decide between you and me; and may He see and plead my cause and deliver me from your hand." (1 Sam. 24:10–15)

Saul's response to David indicated an honest but short-lived admission:

> "You are more righteous than I; for you have dealt well with me, while I have dealt wickedly with you. You have declared today that you have done good to me, that the LORD delivered me into your hand and yet you did not kill me." (1 Sam. 24:17–18)

Of course, Saul's ill-motivated pursuit of David did not end there. But, ultimately, Saul would take his own life in a moment of military defeat. David went on to become the greatest king in Israel's history. His journey culminated in a final chorus of praise to God and a legacy that lives on powerfully today (see 1 Chron. 29:10–22).

In his book about the lives of Saul, David, and Absalom, *A Tale of Three Kings*, Gene Edwards expresses the heart of David's cave contemplation in these words:

> Better he kill me than I learn his ways. Better he kill me than
> I become as he is. I shall not practice the ways that cause kings
> to go mad. I will not throw spears, nor will I allow hatred
> to grow in my heart. I will not avenge. I will not destroy the
> Lord's anointed. Not now. Not ever![4]

Choosing a Good Testimony

Here we see a helpful portrait of an unshaken life. We can have a heart that trusts God's justice and providence rather than our human instinct to get revenge or enact some nuance of evil. This is in stark contrast to our cultural disposition that glibly declares, "I don't get mad; I just get even."

Solomon could have reflected on the legendary accounts of his dad when he wrote, "Deceit is in the heart of those who devise evil, but counselors of peace have joy" (Prov. 12:20). And then again, "Will they not go astray who devise evil? But kindness and truth will be to those who devise good" (Prov. 14:22).

Maybe even now, you are struggling with the secret stirrings of what God would classify as an evil response toward someone you love—or someone you are trying not to hate. I've been there too. Maybe too often. All of us have. Yet here is the advice that we desperately need to embrace:

> Never pay back evil for evil to anyone. Respect what is right
> in the sight of all men. If possible, so far as it depends on
> you, be at peace with all men. Never take your own revenge,
> beloved, but leave room for the wrath of God, for it is writ-
> ten, "Vengeance is Mine, I will repay," says the Lord. "But if

your enemy is hungry, feed him, and if he is thirsty, give him a drink; for in so doing you will heap burning coals on his head." Do not be overcome by evil, but overcome evil with good. (Rom. 12:17–21)

A few key observations help us apply this truth:

Resolve, Don't React

By God's grace and the power of the Holy Spirit, we can resist the urge for payback. Rather than a combative response, we can resolve to take a peaceable posture. I remember listening to a stand-up comedian talking about the wisdom he learned from his dad when reacting to his wife. The fatherly wisdom was, "Say the third thing that comes to your mind." In other words, the first thing that hits your brain during an emotionally charged interaction will probably not be helpful. The second one will likely create more problems. However, by the time you process your response, the third expression might be safe. The advice was humorous but also helpful.

> THE FIRST THING THAT HITS YOUR BRAIN DURING AN EMOTIONALLY CHARGED INTERACTION WILL PROBABLY NOT BE HELPFUL.

Pursue Peace, Not Perfection

Notice the caveat in this verse: "If possible, so far as it depends on you, be at peace with all men" (Rom. 12:18). If possible. Granted, some people will never reciprocate our goodness and attempts for peace. Evil, bitterness, and obstinance may continue to dominate the hearts and minds of people in our orbit. But we can pursue peace believing that "the seed whose fruit is righteousness is sown in peace by those who make peace" (James 3:18).

Trust God, Not Your Instincts

The apostle Paul urges, "Never take your own revenge, beloved, but leave room for the wrath of God" (Rom. 12:19). We are all driven toward self-justification. Our competitive streak wants to win the final argument. We want to look back at our defeated relational foes feeling the "thrill of victory." But we are commanded to leave it in the Lord's hands by placing our lives in the hands of God. We can trust the final judgment rather than spend our energies engaging our enemies.

As I was preparing to write this chapter this morning, I was drawn again to Psalm 3, which is marked as another song David composed after being betrayed and exiled by Absalom. It opens with the refrain:

O Lord, how my adversaries have increased! Many are rising
up against me. Many are saying of my soul, "There is no
deliverance for him in God." But You, O Lord, are a shield
about me, my glory, and the One who lifts my head. I was
crying to the Lord with my voice, and He answered me
from His holy mountain. (Ps. 3:1–4)

David's choice to trust God gripped my heart. When overwhelmed by opponents or simmering with frustration, God can give the grace to say, "But You, O Lord, are a shield about me, my glory, and the One who lifts my head."

At the end of the psalm, David recognized the evil that was taking place against him, but he trusted God to act on his behalf—to judge the wicked and deliver his soul.

Arise, O Lord; save me, O my God! For You have smitten
all my enemies on the cheek; You have shattered the teeth of
the wicked. Salvation belongs to the Lord; Your blessing be
upon Your people! (Ps. 3:7–8)

By faith, he believed God would act in his defense. Notice the line: "Your blessing be upon Your people!" The kingdom over which David reigned was not comprised of his people, but God's. Thousands of these people were caught up in the conspiracy of the moment. Perhaps God was giving David grace to experience Romans 12:14: "Bless those who persecute you; bless and do not curse." Either way, we see the purity and goodness of David's righteous response to a barrage of agonizing rejection. He does no evil to his neighbor.

Pursue Goodness to Overcome Evil

Romans 12:21 unleashes a powerful command: "Do not be overcome by evil, but overcome evil with good." Paul wrote similarly to the Thessalonians, "See that no one repays another with evil for evil, but always seek after that which is good for one another and for all people" (1 Thess. 5:15). The elderly apostle John also affirmed, "Beloved, do not imitate what is evil, but what is good. The one who does good is of God; the one who does evil has not seen God" (3 John 11). The mark of one who knows God and lives an unshaken life is that they do good in the face of evil.

We live in an evil world. We have heard about the Holocaust, the destruction of entire tribes, and other atrocities throughout the world and history. We follow news stories of senseless acts of murder. We read about corruption at almost every level of government and in countless business boardrooms.

Closer to home, Christians are being maligned and misrepresented by antagonistic opponents of all that is good. And, getting personal, you can probably picture the faces of some folks who are inflicting misery on you.

Here is some great news. It is likely to get worse: "Indeed, all who desire to live godly in Christ Jesus will be persecuted. But evil men and impostors will proceed from bad to worse, deceiving and being deceived" (2 Tim. 3:12–13).

So how do we overcome evil with good? Here are a few obvious choices we can make every day:

Pray for Evildoers – David did this. "In return for my love they act as my accusers; but I am in prayer" (Ps. 109:4). Jesus commanded this: "But I say to you, love your enemies and pray for those who persecute you, so that you may be sons of your Father who is in heaven" (Matt. 5:44–45). Our prayers may not change the evildoers, but they will change us. We will prove to be children of the Father.

Live a Life of Light – In the physical world, light always overcomes darkness. Our problem today is not the darkness's pervasiveness but our failure to display the light. God calls us to live as "children of God above reproach in the midst of a crooked and perverse generation, among whom you appear as lights in the world" (Phil. 2:15).

Exhibit a Heart of Honor – To persecuted believers in the first century, Peter wrote, "For such is the will of God that by doing right you may silence the ignorance of foolish men. Act as free men, and do not use your freedom as a covering for evil, but use it as bondslaves of God. Honor all people, love the brotherhood, fear God, honor the king" (1 Peter 2:15–17). Honor is a testimony of the power of godliness. It is a resolve against which there is no defense, even in the face of a hostile culture.

> OUR PROBLEM TODAY IS NOT THE DARKNESS'S PERVASIVENESS BUT THE LIGHT'S FAILURE.

Trust Your Trustworthy God – David trusted God in his darkest moments of treachery. He set his heart on God's unchanging character and His power to change David's character. You can do the same.

I began this chapter by recounting one of my most painful moments in life and ministry. In truth, it was a difficult season that spanned four years. I came close to walking away from vocational ministry. Toward the end of that ministry chapter, our wise and caring elders sent Rosemary and me to a retreat center for hurting ministry couples. Over a span of ten days, we received wise counsel, helpful healing, and fresh hope to remain in pastoral ministry for decades to come. Over the years I have been privileged to speak to many pastors at conferences and coach many of them personally. As He often does, God redeemed my most painful moments to give me the most fruitful ministry to others who encounter hurts and heartaches along the way.

The great lesson learned through it all was that I have to choose what I will trust every day. I can trust what I feel in my emotions, which is unreliable. I can trust what I see with my eyes, which is superficial and temporal. Or I can choose what I know to be true about God's truth and character.

So, for me, the situation looked bad, and felt bad. But I chose to trust that God was good. Those days, and some days even now, felt and looked out of control. But I decided to trust that God was sovereign. There were many ways that season felt and looked very unfair. But I chose to believe that God was just—both in the moment and in eternity.

David made a similar choice in the pit of despair. So can you. As a result, you will overcome every fleshly impulse to do evil to your neighbor—and will live in the promise of a never-shaken life—trusting a God who is sovereign, just, and good.

Never Shaken Application

- Pinpoint a situation where you were tempted to react in a way that would have been hurtful to another person. What did you do? What was the outcome? What did you learn from this experience that can help you to respond differently today?

- Review Romans 12:17–21. In what way do you feel you can most helpfully apply the truths found here? Thinking about the week ahead of you, pray now for help from the Spirit of God to respond accordingly.
- As you reflect on what has been said in this chapter about overcoming evil with good, what do you suppose David needed to do in his situation? What specific circumstance in your life will give you an opportunity to practice this biblical approach?

Chapter 8

STOP THE SPREAD

Nor takes up a reproach against his friend . . .

PSALM 15:3

Always remember . . . rumors are carried by haters,
spread by fools, and accepted by idiots.

ZIAD K. ABDELNOUR

One evening as we were casually hanging out at my daughter and son-in-law's home, we began to share some of the more recent Christian songs we were currently enjoying. She told me of the new album from a very well-known Christian recording artist. I immediately retorted, "I stopped listening to him. He had an affair, left his wife, and got a divorce. He's lost all credibility." She responded in complete disbelief, wisely questioning what I had just announced. So, naturally, we Googled it. I tried several variations of words, searching the internet for some report to underscore the disdain I had harbored for over a year.

To my surprise, I found nothing. The only data I unearthed spoke of his marriage, love for his wife, and his role as a faithful father. I was humiliated by my long-held assumptions. I was embarrassed about my bias. My daughter asked, "Where did you get that idea?" My response was embarrassing. "Someone told me." When she asked who, I could not even remember. Lesson learned. Since then, we have gone together to two of his concerts. His incredible music and solid gospel-centered lyrics have blessed my heart countless times in recent years.

The Inflow of the Verbal Sewer Line

David's inspired song has affirmed to our hearts these essential truths: "He does not slander with his tongue, nor does evil to his neighbor, nor takes up a reproach against his friend" (Ps. 15:3). You could say that David unpacked the meat in this relationship sandwich in the previous chapter. We refrain from any evil toward those in our lives. The two pieces of bread in this sandwich have to do with words. Slanderous words spoken and derogatory words received. While others may be the lord of their tongue, I must also be the master of my ears.

Who knows all the questionable and undermining expressions Absalom might have shared during the days that he sat at the city gates, garnering loyalty to himself at his father's expense (2 Sam. 15:2–6)? "David doesn't really care about you because . . ." "Did you hear what David did?" "Someone told me that David said . . ." Having an audience, Absalom kept talking. The vulnerable audience pondered his words. The internal thoughts and public opinion toward David began to mutate. Soon, this stirred the will of enough compliant participants to bring it all to a tipping point. Absalom's rebellion had fermented long enough to become a reality.

> **WHILE OTHERS MAY BE THE LORD OF THEIR TONGUE, I MUST ALSO BE THE MASTER OF MY EARS.**

So David, banished to the wilderness, continues his song. It likely had melancholy tones but was packed with ever-deepening conviction. "If I am a true worshiper, if I want an unshakable life—I must play by God's rules. I cannot take up a reproach against a friend." No matter how normal or natural it seems, God tells us to guard our ears.

To "take up" simply means to receive, to endure, or to accept as accurate. In the Hebrew, you find that it is the same word used in Numbers 21 when the bronze serpent was "lifted up." So, we don't receive nor do we elevate to others the flaws or failings of a friend.

The heart of this verse is that we will not give attention to critical tidbits about someone, and we refuse to carry it any further. Today, it is just the way we roll—in politics, business, and even in families. We love to hear the juicy stuff. The bombastic captures our attention. We find a twisted secret pleasure in being "in the know" about the latest gossip. But the Bible warns, "You shall not bear a false report; do not join your hand with a wicked man to be a malicious witness" (Ex. 23:1).

> **RUMORS CAN DESTROY RELATIONSHIPS, CREATE UPHEAVAL IN CHURCHES, AND UNDERMINE OUR GOSPEL TESTIMONY.**

Social media serves as a global pipeline for communication that is suspect. Fact-checker sites need other fact-checker sites to check their "facts." Group text threads carry the potential to weave tales of mystery and mischief.

Words, in whatever form, are potent. Rumors can destroy relationships, create upheaval in churches, and undermine our gospel testimony. Just as David's city had been divided through the spread of whispers, rumors, and innuendos, so it happens today.

Stepping Out of Line

Practically all of us have at one time played the game "Telephone." Players form a line or circle. The first player thinks of some phrase or idea and whispers it to the next person in the line. The second person whispers what they think they heard to the third in line. This process continues until the last person declares the message that has typically morphed via the numerous whisperings. The fun is in hearing the difference between the last statement and the first.[1]

In real life, we replicate this process. In an ideal world, person five would immediately step out of the line, walk back to the guy in the front who started the conversation and directly verify the accuracy and truth of what was said. Because, in the real world, listening to and passing on juicy whisperings about someone is not funny. It is hurtful and destructive.

When we take up a reproach against a friend, we have become part of the problem. More concerning is that our willingness to even remain in the line of skewed reporting may reveal something serious about our own hearts. As Paul Tripp explains,

> The love of controversy demeans people down to your prey, not human beings made in the holy image of God. If they're outside of the community of faith, they cease to be a lost soul in need of rescue; they're a target. If they're a brother or sister in Christ, what now gives you joy is not the messy process of love but the challenge of knocking someone down.[2]

Not only does our tongue reveal our troubled heart condition (as we saw in chapter 6) but even our ears can be a revelation of our need to "speak the truth in our heart" (chapter 5) and repent over a love of controversy.

Polluted Airwaves

A "reproach" or a "slur" (NIV) is something negative that is cast upon another. It includes the placing of blame, the pinning of guilt, or the questioning of character. Innuendos come floating your way, just waiting for you to make your ears a garbage dump for what others are distributing.

In daily relationships, we encounter people whose philosophy is, "If you can't say anything good about someone . . . then let's hear it!" They seem to have a fascination with the rumor mill. They find some twisted delight in hearing the latest rumors or unverified stories about others.

People who spread rumors seldom bother to determine if there is any truth to what they are saying. The lead-in lines often sound like,

"Did you hear the latest?" or "I'm not sure this is true but . . ." or "Someone told me . . ." One expert notes,

> This is the power of rumor and innuendo. You can lead people to certain conclusions through suggestions and partial information. Once they have followed the implications to the obvious conclusion, that conclusion will *stick*. Discrediting the incorrect rumors and providing more complete information isn't enough to get people to change their beliefs.[3]

Once embedded in the mind and indulged for a while, ideas are often hard to shake. Proverbs 26:22 affirms, "The words of a whisperer are like dainty morsels, and they go down into the innermost parts of the body." Likewise, Psalm 15 teaches that the firm of character might be subject to listening to "dainty morsels." Still, they refuse to believe it or pass it on until, through a biblical process, they are persuaded that it's true.

DISCERNING TRUTH, GOSSIP, AND WHEN TO SHARE

Is it true?

Yes	Unsure	No
If you are not part of the problem or the solution, then seek to confirm with someone else who is. Request they follow a biblical process of confrontation and restoration.	Resolve to discreetly discover any pertinent facts from those directly involved. Once determined, seek to advance a biblical process initiated by those closest to the situation.	Shut the conversation down. Confront the person about the destructive nature of gossip.

Does it involve someone I know?

Yes	No
Go directly to the person(s) involved to see how you can help by gaining clarification or providing needed confrontation.	Possibly seek out another person who knows them and request that they go directly to clarify or help.

Is it necessary to share this information?	
Yes	**No**
If your participation is loving and necessary for resolution, justice, or the safety for those involved.	If your involvement is not helpful to advance any resolution or might involve the spreading of gossip.

Do I have godly motives for sharing this information?		
Yes	**Unsure**	**No**
Resolve to seek illumination and restoration via a biblical process.	Pray and seek godly counsel—not mentioning names but just evaluating your own heart in the matter.	Remove yourself from any conversation or discussion. Address the issues of your own heart first (*i.e.,* anger, jealousy, unforgiveness, etc.).

A Lionhearted Strategy

A less-famous story of *Aesop's Fables* tells of the scheme of a lion who eventually figured out how to make four fabulous meals out of a quartet of bulls—a single serving at a time.

> Once on a time four Bulls agreed
> To herd together and to feed
> In the same pasture. Crouched near by,
> A Lion watched, but dared not try
> His strength against four Bulls combined:
> And so by craft he undermined
> Their friendship, sowing seeds of hate
> And causing them to separate
> And graze in fields apart. This done,
> He feasted on them one by one.[4]

We don't know exactly how the lion undermined their bond of friendship, but we learn that he sowed "seeds of hate." Maybe when one would fall behind, he would sneak up and whisper, "The other three are talking about you behind your back," or "They are out to get you," or "You can't trust Bull #2 because he is a thief and a liar. Keep your distance." In any case, it worked. It still works today.

Staying in the animal kingdom for a moment, Proverbs 26:17 illustrates, "Like one who takes a dog by the ears is he who passes by and meddles with strife not belonging to him." So don't be a bull who is taken out by the latest verbal garbage. Don't get bitten by a mad dog by grabbing the "ears" of some rumor or babbling buzz that seeks to catch your attention.

Fiery Potential

Recently, we were visiting with my son and his family. As we casually shopped at Sam's Club, he received a call from his best friend who was out of town. This friend had just received a call from his son saying a small fire had started in the garage of his home. My son and I immediately jumped in the car and drove speedily to the house, just five minutes away. We arrived before the fire department. As we drove onto the property, we saw flames dancing violently from the house's roof. Within minutes, the entire structure was engulfed. All the fire department could do was to try and minimize the damage. Sadly, the home was destroyed. You may have witnessed or even experienced this kind of tragedy as well.

A canyon in Butte County, California, became suddenly enflamed one morning in November 2018. The spark that created the "Camp Fire" soon became the costliest natural disaster worldwide that year. It remains the most deadly and destructive wildfire in California history. One expert explained, "A house fire can go from an incipient (just starting) fire to a fully involved [fire] in as little as 4–5 minutes. A forest fire or wildfire can spread as quickly as an acre per second!"[5]

In more recent news, the world watched in horror when the Lahaina fire swept through the historic Hawaiian community on the island of Maui. Drought conditions and sixty-seven-mile-an-hour winds accelerated the sudden destruction that resulted in $3.2 billion in losses, burning 2,170 acres, and damaging or destroying three thousand structures, many of them composed of older, wood frame construction.[6] Around a hundred people died and dozens remained missing weeks later.[7]

The Bible asserts that the tongue is a fire. "A worthless man digs up evil, while his words are like scorching fire" (Prov. 16:27). James warns that a "forest is set aflame by such a small fire! And the tongue is a fire, the very world of iniquity; the tongue is set among our members as that which defiles the entire body, and sets on fire the course of our life, and is set on fire by hell" (James 3:5–6). Talk about a clear and present danger!

When the rumor mill is active, flames are dancing dangerously in the atmosphere. Sparks are wafting through the air. So, here is an "extinguisher" that might keep you from "taking up a reproach against a friend." The next time someone approaches you, like a lion to a bull, yell "Fire!" (unless you're in a crowded theater). I guarantee they will remove you from their gossip chain after that riveting encounter. The reality is that anytime someone approaches us with the latest "word on the street," we are going to pour water or gas on that verbal fire by how we respond.

Reframing the commentary from above on the wildfires in California and Maui, here is the point: Fueled by hearts that have tolerated a drought of the Word of God and propelled by powerful gusts of carnality, the verbal flames move swiftly. In less than twenty-four hours, the fire can sweep through churches and circles of friends, leaving charred and ruined relationships in its wake.

Limiting Your Intake

Here is more practical advice (and less dramatic than yelling "Fire!"). To become people who are not safe to those who want to spread a questionable word in our direction, Jon Bloom advises that we immediately ask these questions:

- "Have you shared your concern with this person directly? I'd be willing to go with you to talk to him."
- "Just to be clear, is this information I should know? Do you want me to help you pursue reconciliation?"
- "Are you doing everything you possibly can to put away 'all bitterness and wrath and anger and clamor and slander'? (Ephesians 4:31)"
- "How can I help you guard this person's reputation like a treasure? (Proverbs 22:1)"[8]

> THE MORE WE FILL OUR MINDS WITH THE BEST THINGS OF GOD'S INFALLIBLE AND TRANSFORMING WORD (ROM. 12:1–2), THE LESS VULNERABLE THEY WILL BE TO QUESTIONABLE INFORMATION INFECTIONS.

He notes that friends don't let friends slander. Someone who passes on gossip to you will soon pass on gossip about you. It is in everyone's best interest to take a sledgehammer to the rumor mill.

A Never-Shaken Mind

It's been said that a mind is a terrible thing to waste. It is also a terrible thing to pollute our minds with waste. So another essential reason to not "take up a reproach against a friend" is simply to guard your mind. Philippians 4:8 offers powerful guidance:

Finally, brethren, whatever is true, whatever is honorable, whatever is right, whatever is pure, whatever is lovely, whatever is of good repute, if there is any excellence and if anything worthy of praise, dwell on these things.

Negativity is sticky in the brain. Ungodly verbal viruses infect our thoughts with damaging ideas that need to be treated with the cure of biblical truth. The more we fill our minds with the best things of

God's infallible and transforming Word (Rom. 12:1–2), the less vulnerable they will be to questionable information infections. A healthy and holy mind makes for a stable life. We are never shaken.

Spreading Beyond Repair

A story is told of an extraordinary penance enacted by a sixteenth-century Catholic priest named Philip Neri. He was advising a remorseful woman regarding her sin of "taking up a reproach" and then spreading it around. Neri instructed her to implement an unusual demonstration of repentance. He requested that she find a feather pillow and climb to the top of the church bell tower. Following his instruction, she then ripped it open, allowing the wind to blow countless feathers all across the local area.

> **WHEN MALIGNANT WORDS ARE SCATTERED ABROAD, IT CAN BE IMPOSSIBLE TO GATHER THEM BACK. THEY CONTINUE TO DISHONOR AND DIVIDE FOR DAYS, MONTHS, AND YEARS.**

The wise priest then gave her a second and more difficult task. He told her to go about the area, gathering all the scattered feathers in order to put them back in the pillow. Of course, the humbled lady knew this was impossible. Neri's unorthodox assignment clearly and dramatically underscored the destructive nature of her gossip.[9]

Classified Information

In recent years, news headlines have been dominated by the mishandling of classified documents by high-profile politicians. In each case, it involves sensitive information that must be protected as determined by an official government body in the collective best interest of a just society, its people, and its national defense. There are various levels of classification, like top secret, secret, and confidential. Each has the potential to cause danger to national concerns with an unauthorized release.[10]

As we have seen, any decision to inappropriately entertain private (aka classified) information about a friend, work associate, church member, church leader, community leader, or even a politician can cause grave damage. When malignant words are scattered abroad, it can be impossible to gather them back. They continue to dishonor and divide for days, months, and years. Questions and flawed conclusions linger in people's minds and pass from one talebearer to the next. Therefore, Christians of character avoid the discovery and dissemination of classified personal reports.

The Security of Holy Friendships

You may not have a tendency to outright slander people. Still, Psalm 15:3 challenges us just as seriously to avoid the sinful trap of opening our ears and hearts to the wrong stuff. Yes, it is an issue of character. It is the pathway to healthy and holy friendships. It is a recipe for absolute security and strength in your relational network.

Proverbs 22:11 promises, "He who loves purity of heart and whose speech is gracious, the king is his friend." A gracious reputation and favor with others are the fruit of guarded ears. Since lip and ear management are ultimately a heart issue, we can embrace the promise of Jesus with renewed desire, "Blessed are the pure in heart, for they shall see God" (Matt. 5:8). In another parallel song, David identified those who would "ascend into the hill of the LORD" and "stand in His holy place"—similar to the intimacy with God that Jesus promised. David describes this person as "he who has clean hands and a pure heart, who has not lifted up his soul to falsehood and has not sworn deceitfully" (Ps. 24:3–4).

So the "never-shaken" plan is clear. Speak no evil. Do no evil. Listen to no evil. Be careful, little ears, what you hear. Stop the spread.

Never Shaken Application

- Have you ever heard and believed something about another person, only to discover later that it was not true? How did this occur, and what was the outcome? How might you avoid this in the future?
- Review the truth of Philippians 4:8. How will these areas of focus better guard your ears and mind from taking in things that might be harmful in some way? Consider a specific relational environment where this might be a temptation. What specific truth in this verse might prove to be most helpful?
- What practical applications from this chapter will help you respond more appropriately the next time someone approaches you with an expression that would be derogatory toward another? Pray now in advance that you can be prepared and principled in your reaction.

Chapter 9

GODLINESS BY ASSOCIATION

In whose eyes a reprobate is despised,
But who honors those who fear the LORD.

PSALM 15:4

The starting points of character and destiny in the young
begin with home environment and outside associations.

HENRY F. BANKS

When our children were growing up, we implemented many of the typical rhythms Christian parents embrace. First, we tried to model the Christian life in our home by our own devotion, extending that to "family devotions." We took them to church (which wasn't a choice since I was the pastor). I journaled for each of them, tracking some of their significant experiences and lessons. They have these journals today. We developed twelve "family principles" that we reviewed regularly.[1] All three of our kids had a balanced exposure in their educational journey, experiencing homeschooling, Christian school, and public school. We prayed for them and with them. They accompanied me on various overseas missions trips when they were each ten years old.

Today, they are all married to devoted Christ followers. As of this writing, each family is in full-time ministry. They have also blessed us with eleven truly amazing grandchildren.

To help create vital guardrails, we selected some crucial memory verses we regularly reviewed. One of those Scriptures was "he who walks with wise men will be wise, but the companion of fools will suffer harm" (Prov. 13:20). We knew that the friendships and interests our children formed were wild cards in the deck that would have significant impact on their spiritual life and well-being.

This proved to be the Achilles' heel in our parenting journey. There were times when we had the impression that a friend was a decent kid. We were told that a friend's parents were good Christians. You know how it goes. Some of these less suspicious connections proved to be a snare to a child and a source of great heartache for us as the ramifications of these friendships played out.

Shaped by Association

Charles "Tremendous" Jones, a chapel speaker during my college years, stated a truth that I wrote down and have not forgotten: "You will be the same person in five years as you are today except for the people you associate with and the books you read." These days, it is more complicated. We could expand "the books you read" to include the apps you download, the television series you watch, the social media influencers you follow, and more. The options for the input that shape our thoughts and values seem endless.

For children today, it now includes the video games they play, the TikTok or YouTube videos they watch, the musical artists they love, the concerts they attend, the values they are taught at school, and the sports heroes they idolize.

Of all these "influencers" for young and old, the personal, relational association factor runs strong. Friends, office connections, shopping partners, golf buddies, college roommates—all can have a subtle but substantive impact on our values and worldview. When your kids go to school tomorrow or hang out with the friend down the street, they will likely be surrounded by persuasive peers who have swallowed today's morally depraved bait—hook, line, and sinker.

Friends That Facilitate a Downfall

We come to another key principle of an unshaken life. "In whose eyes a reprobate is despised, but who honors those who fear the LORD" (Ps. 15:4). A kaleidoscope of questionable alliances and evil associations had led to David's demise. Absalom and other influencers had compromised integrity to create a united rebellion. God reminded David: others may compromise, but you must not.

This principle of rejecting the vile rascals of life and instead admiring truly decent people (and practices) is easier said than done in this world. Our insecure hearts want to be accepted by the "in" crowd. The deceiver Satan unleashes all of his most illusory weapons to attract our hearts toward that superficial call of this world's good life. We are foolishly fascinated by the veneer of the "rich and famous," failing to discern their below-the-surface misery and their hopeless eternal destiny. Just as the luscious allure of the forbidden fruit of Eden gave the serpent an avenue to confuse the truth and deceive the mind of Eve, so we are enticed to confusion and compromise by the fascination of life on the other side of the moral tracks.

Easier Said Than Done

David's son Solomon wrote often about this principle. For instance,

> Do not enter the path of the wicked and do not proceed in the way of evil men. (Prov. 4:14)

> Do not eat the bread of a selfish man, or desire his delicacies. (Prov. 23:6)

> Do not let your heart envy sinners, but live in the fear of the LORD always. Surely there is a future, and your hope will not be cut off. (Prov. 23:17–18)

Do not be envious of evil men, nor desire to be with them.
(Prov. 24:1)

Easier said than done. If you know Solomon's journey you know that he controverted much of the wisdom God had inspired in him during the earlier days. He started well and ended miserably. Instead of despising evil and honoring the good, he honored other gods, loved pagan women, and rejected God in his final chapters of life.

Now King Solomon loved many foreign women along with the daughter of Pharaoh: Moabite, Ammonite, Edomite, Sidonian, and Hittite women, from the nations concerning which the Lord had said to the sons of Israel, "You shall not associate with them, nor shall they associate with you, for they will surely turn your heart away after their gods." Solomon held fast to these in love. He had seven hundred wives, princesses, and three hundred concubines, and his wives turned his heart away. For when Solomon was old, his wives turned his heart away after other gods; and his heart was not wholly devoted to the Lord his God, as the heart of David his father had been.
(1 Kings 11:1–4)

Take heed. If it can happen to him, it can happen to you and me. "Do not be deceived: 'Bad company corrupts good morals'" (1 Cor. 15:33). The security and strength of an unshaken life can evaporate because of the choices we make. The downward slide often happens one relationship at a time, one impulse of interest at a time.

The Standard and Outcome of All Things Vile

Psalm 15:4 says, "In whose eyes a reprobate is despised." Other translations describe this as a "vile person" (esv), "flagrant sinner" (nlt), and "one rejected by the Lord" (hcsb). What seems harsh is abundantly clear. Today, innumerable flagrant sinners call for the attention and admiration of the masses. You may not want to label them as such on social media, but we must understand who they are. Rather than feeling any sense of attraction or admiration, we must actually "despise" their values and behaviors.

"Reprobate" (NASB) literally refers to someone who is "rejected" or "cast off" by a holy God. Our view and value of this person must agree with God's, not the opinion of the Grammys, Oscars, or ESPY Awards. Our esteem is not based on the number of social media followers but by the degree to which they are God followers. Frankly, these characters need to be absent from our homes, minds, and value system. Our music playlists, our favorite movies, and our close circle of influencers should be screened according to Psalm 15:4.

In the New Testament, these people are described with the kind of raw detail that is sadly reflected in today's news and social media.

> For this reason God gave them over to degrading passions; for their women exchanged the natural function for that which is unnatural, and in the same way also the men abandoned the natural function of the woman and burned in their desire toward one another, men with men committing indecent acts and receiving in their own persons the due penalty of their error.
>
> And just as they did not see fit to acknowledge God any longer, God gave them over to a depraved mind, to do those things which are not proper, being filled with all unrighteousness, wickedness, greed, evil; full of envy, murder, strife, deceit, malice; they are gossips, slanderers, haters of God, insolent, arrogant, boastful, inventors of evil, disobedient to parents, without understanding, untrustworthy, unloving, unmerciful; and although they know the ordinance of God, that those who practice such things are worthy of death, they

not only do the same, but also give hearty approval to those who practice them. (Rom. 1:26–32)

> WE SHOULD SEE THEM AS *VICTIMS OF* THE ENEMY, NOT *AS* THE ENEMY.

As distasteful (and common) as these behaviors are, we should humbly recognize our own vulnerability to these or similar sins. We should thank God daily for the grace that keeps us in the faith and calls us to a holy life. We certainly can hope and pray for the eternal salvation of the lost, asking God for opportunities to give loving and bold witness for the gospel. We should see them as *victims of* the enemy, not *as* the enemy. We resolve to live as salt and light in hopes of their transformation. But we do not give them honor.

From the Eyes to Emotion to Entrapment

Did you notice the reference to "eyes"? "In whose *eyes* a reprobate is despised" (Ps. 15:4). The eye is often the avenue through which our affections are excited. Inevitably our soul decides to either wisely reject aberrant deceptions or to foolishly honor the dishonorable. All the way back to our original maternal ancestor, Eve, we see this truth.

> When the woman *saw* that the tree was good for food, and that it was a delight to the *eyes*, and that the tree was desirable to make one wise, she took from its fruit and ate; and she gave also to her husband with her, and he ate. (Gen. 3:6)

Solomon's gaze became fixed on the beauty of foreign women. He no longer despised false religion but became a dishonor to those who truly feared the Lord.

The psalmist Asaph records his journey of agonizing doubt and despair in Psalm 73. He eventually "entered the sanctuary of God"

(v. 17 NIV) and regained holy, healthy perspective. His description of the initial downward spiral explains, "I was envious of the arrogant as I saw the prosperity of the wicked" (Ps. 73:3).

Remember that Absalom was extremely good looking, had long flowing hair, and was persuasive and charming. These optics added to his convincing influence as he sought to allure the hearts of Jerusalem's gullible citizens away from David and toward his devious schemes.

Our world is more "visual" than ever. TikTok, YouTube, video games, television ads, and even good old magazine covers at the checkout stand seek to rivet our eyes and grab our hearts away from a lifestyle of properly fixed honor. Add the hypersexualized advertising of the day with the onslaught of readily available pornography, and the battle for honor is exponentially severe. Of course, in countless ways, our children and grandchildren are the strategic targets of this influence. Parental guidance and guardrails really matter in today's world.

A Game Plan for Life-Advancing Honor

We now come to our single-minded pursuit. The never-shaken life "honors those who fear the LORD." To honor is to go out of your way to make someone honorable, to lift them up, to elevate them, to esteem them highly. Honor must be proactive and intentional. We cannot leave an "honor vacuum" in our mind and soul. We must fill it with an understanding of "the fear of the LORD" and deliberately esteem those who reflect this kind of character.

Those who "fear the LORD" are best described in Proverbs 9:10: "The fear of the LORD is the beginning of wisdom, and the knowledge of the Holy One is understanding." You can probably think of some names and faces even now. These are the people in our lives who are consistently wise and obedient because of their genuine reverence for Christ. They could be members of your immediate and extended family. You know them as leaders at church, workers on the job, first responders, coaches, teachers, and even some politicians, actors, and sports figures. Here is the bottom line: make every effort to give them a place of honor in your heart, words, and actions. Fill the void with honor so there is no room for or interest in lesser things.

Heroes and Models Matter

Fred Smith wrote in his book *You and Your Network* that heroes are the personification of our ideals, the embodiment of our highest values. "A society writes its diary by naming its heroes. We as individuals do the same. When Socrates said, 'Talk, young man, that I might know you,' he could have also added, 'Talk of your heroes that I might know not only who you are, but who you will become.'"[2]

The heroes we honor can be found in Scripture, church history, biographies, and in some stories of our day. Models, on the other hand, are those who fear the Lord and with whom we have a relationship. Smith again clarifies,

> While our heroes inspire us to *be*, our models help us to *do*.
> . . . Heroes we idolize and models we emulate. A person is
> easier to emulate than an essay. We are able to query our
> models and share in the dynamism that drives them. We
> borrow from their motivation.[3]

In today's world, celebrities and social media influencers may dazzle us (or our children), but God-fearing heroes and models will inspire and enlarge us.

Morris Massey, in his book *The People Puzzle*, makes the case that the heroes a child embraces at ten years old provide a vital clue to who that child will become. He concludes from his studies that children look around for others whose lives are attractive to them. Those individuals become their role models.[4]

For many years, I had a dozen framed pictures on my office wall of those who have most influenced me. Included in the gallery were my parents, in-laws, an older brother, and a number of pastors who had shaped my life and ministry. Under each picture I listed two or three key character traits. This was my wall of honor, reminding me of what I really valued and who I hoped to become.

The more we honor the honorable, the clearer we discern the emptiness and foolishness of the dishonorable. We desperately need selective vision, discerning minds, and guarded hearts as we navigate this upside-down culture. Conversely, we must elevate and actively engage in the honor due to those who fear the Lord.

Honor Begins at Home

The household is the initial epicenter of a culture of Christian honor. First Peter 3:7 states, "You husbands in the same way, live with your wives in an understanding way, as with someone weaker, since she is a woman; and show her honor as a fellow heir of the grace of life, so that your prayers will not be hindered." The preceding verses also describe how wives can honor their husband. Perhaps honor is more caught than taught. Children will instinctively honor those who fear the Lord when they see it in the living laboratory of home life.

> **THE MORE WE HONOR THE HONORABLE, THE CLEARER WE DISCERN THE EMPTINESS AND FOOLISHNESS OF THE DISHONORABLE.**

Of course, the Ten Commandments and New Testament teachings affirm this homegrown honor. "Honor your father and mother" (Ex. 20:12; Eph. 6:2). Honor begets honor. This honor for parents, many of whom have quirks and imperfections, extends throughout adult life. One of *Grimms' Fairy Tales* illustrates this:

> There was once a very old man, whose eyes had become
> dim, his ears dull of hearing, his knees trembled, and when

he sat at table he could hardly hold the spoon, and spilt the broth upon the table-cloth or let it run out of his mouth. His son and his son's wife were disgusted at this, so the old grandfather at last had to sit in the corner behind the stove, and they gave him his food in an earthenware bowl, and not even enough of it. And he used to look towards the table with his eyes full of tears. Once, too, his trembling hands could not hold the bowl, and it fell to the ground and broke. The young wife scolded him, but he said nothing and only sighed. Then they bought him a wooden bowl for a few half-pence, out of which he had to eat. They were once sitting thus when the little grandson of four years old began to gather together some bits of wood upon the ground. "What are you doing there?" asked the father. "I am making a little trough," answered the child, "for father and mother to eat out of when I am big."

The man and his wife looked at each other for a while, and presently began to cry. Then they took the old grandfather to the table, and henceforth always let him eat with them, and likewise said nothing if he did spill a little of anything.[5]

Honor and dishonor are as much caught as taught. They translate in subtle but lifelong ways to those we influence and for generations to come.

The Honor-Filled Church

Romans 12:10 provides a great relational goalpost for all believers: "Be devoted to one another in brotherly love; give preference to one another in honor." Other versions affirm, "Outdo one another in showing honor" (ESV) and "Take delight in honoring each other" (NLT).

James unleashed the inspired and necessary truth when he exposed the tendency to honor the rich over the poor in Christian gatherings by giving special treatment based on the values of the world rather than God's value of every human soul. He observed: "Have you not made distinctions among yourselves, and become judges with evil motives?" (James 2:4). Honor must be based on God-worth, not net worth.

First Corinthians 12 speaks of the necessity of every member of the body of Christ and cautions us about parsing out "honor" based on superficial standards. "Those members of the body which we deem less honorable, on these we bestow more abundant honor, and our less presentable members become much more presentable" (v. 23). So we are called to embrace and express unbiased honor to one another as believers, regardless of any measurements of worldly value. As an application, make it a point this week to find some Christian who may not get much appreciation or esteem and honor them with your words, or some other practical expression of blessing. It will be good for your soul and encourage them in meaningful ways.

Influential Honor in Society

In the strictest sense, our hearts honor those who fear the Lord, but we also exhibit appropriate honor to those in authority as a testimony for the grace of the gospel. First Peter 2:15–17 explains: "For such is the will of God that by doing right you may silence the ignorance of foolish men. Act as free men, and do not use your freedom as a covering for evil, but use it as bondslaves of God. Honor all people, love the brotherhood, fear God, honor the king." That is a tough pill to swallow in many cases. It surely was for believers under godless Roman rulers. But, rooted in our fear of the Lord, we are able to exhibit honor in the toughest of situations without any personal affection for the godless lifestyles they exhibit.

Honor in Our Investments

One additional way we can seek to honor those who fear the Lord is expressed by where we spend and invest our money. Obviously, it is almost impossible to avoid giving our hard-earned dollars to unscrupulous corporations. But we can be wise to seek out businesses that honor Christ and be more intentional in supporting them. The godless of this world make no bones about financially underwriting their anti-Christian causes. We can quietly but intentionally express appropriate honor by withholding our support for corporations that openly oppose biblical morality. Even though it is virtually impossible to accomplish this goal entirely in today's complicated mix of business and entertainment, with a little research and resolve we can at least make an effort to put our money where our morality is. There are sources that can give you guidance in these important spending decisions as an extension of your honor.[6]

Daily Decisions of Honor and Blessing

Perhaps, as David reflected on the pain of his banishment and calculated his next steps for survival, he reminded us of the truth he penned earlier in life:

> I will walk within my house in the integrity of my heart.
> I will set no worthless thing before my eyes; I hate the work
> of those who fall away; it shall not fasten its grip on me.
> . . . My eyes shall be upon the faithful of the land, that they
> may dwell with me; he who walks in a blameless way is the
> one who will minister to me. He who practices deceit shall
> not dwell within my house; he who speaks falsehood shall
> not maintain his position before me. (Ps. 101:2, 3, 6–7)

When compromise might have been calling, David's Psalm 15 song replanted his conviction. He would not fall prey to misplaced honor. He trusted God in his decisions about those with whom he would associate. This became another key ingredient in an unshaken life. The refrain of this promised blessing must have resonated in his heart again:

> How blessed is the man who does not walk in the counsel
> of the wicked, nor stand in the path of sinners, nor sit in the
> seat of scoffers! But his delight is in the law of the LORD, and
> in His law he meditates day and night. He will be like a tree
> firmly planted by streams of water, which yields its fruit in
> its season and its leaf does not wither; and in whatever he
> does, he prospers. (Ps. 1:1–3)

In a recent symposium for church leaders sponsored by our global pastor's fellowship (www.64fellowship.com), a powerful truth captured my heart. In his opening statement, presenter Crawford Loritts explained, "When we are born, we look like our parents. When we die, we look like our decisions."[7] Every day we must decide how we will associate with the network of people in our lives. We must decide who we will honor. David had to make this decision once again.

These consequential associations will shape who we will be five years from now. They will determine who we will be when we die. Make the decision to trust God's promise for an unshaken life. Now go honor some worthy soul!

Never Shaken Application

- In the day-to-day routines of your life, how might you be tempted to give undue attention or honor to "reprobate" people or ideas? What effect might it have on your soul? How can you make adjustments to avoid this propensity?
- As you think of a younger generation (kids, grandkids, etc.), what unique temptations are they facing that might confuse the principles of this chapter? Who are the younger ones in your life, and what will you do to help them make this distinction in order to give more honor to those who fear the Lord?
- As you think of honoring those who fear the Lord, who are your top five? If they are still living, what can you do this week to more actively give them the honor they deserve?

Chapter 10

THE POWER OF A PROMISE KEEPER

He swears to his own hurt and does not change . . .

PSALM 15:4

We live in a time where we can make and break promises with a convenience of a text message. Instead of being encouraged to commit with a "yes" or "no," social media allows us to make half-hearted choices of "interested" or "maybe." Instead of being taught to do all it takes to show up, society gives us permission to keep our options open.

HEIDI TAI

If you were alive and paying attention in the '90s, you will remember the Promise Keepers (or PK as it was popularly called). It started with a relatively small 1991 gathering of around four thousand men at a conference in Colorado. PK would subsequently fill nationwide stadiums featuring high-profile Christian speakers, stirring worship, and a call to keep seven key promises. Then, in 1997, PK drew some 800,000 men to the National Mall in Washington, DC, for "Stand in the Gap: A Sacred Assembly of Men." Reporters tagged this PK event as the second most newsworthy story of 1997.

After the National Mall event in 1997, PK suffered an abrupt decline. The leadership reduced the national staff of 345 to a handful. PK's subsequent gatherings became rare and small. After essentially disappearing from the radar, PK has restructured, refocused, and is seeking to rebound with a new approach, but with the same mission.

In evaluating the roller coaster of PK, one distinguished Christian sociologist and author noted, "In a broader sense, the rise and fall of the Promise Keepers provides insight into American culture. Americans suffer from what might be best described as a collective form of attention deficit disorder."[1] It is true that social enthusiasm for the movement waned and moved on. But, sadly, the spiritual enthusiasm for actually keeping promises seems to be sliding away in today's culture as well.

The mission of PK, whatever your opinion of the movement, struck a chord in the hearts of countless thousands of men. We know that to be never-shaken, we must make godly pledges and keep them. We need to be people of our word. The Bible calls us to this standard, but too often we suffer from attention deficit disorder in our souls. We forget our promises. We move on to the next shiny object that might capture our affection. If we are not careful, we soon are guilty of "commitment deficit disorder."

A Man of His Word

David understood the pain inflicted by broken promises. But whether it was just the fickle nature of a flock of followers or outright denial of personal integrity, David was ousted by a movement of people who changed their minds, shifted their loyalties, and likely chose convenience over character.

In this Psalm 15 moment, his song reflected a powerful refrain. "He swears to his own hurt and does not change" (Ps. 15:4). When his world was sliding away in a sea of fickle commitments, God assured David of the essential character of living as a man of his word.

Living Comfortably with Our Lies

Broken promises abound in today's world. Mainstream behavior compromises truth in countless avenues of human interaction. The guarantees of politicians are disbelieved. The "word" given in a business handshake is often suspect. Parents overpromise with their children. Marriage vows are too often violated. Entrepreneurs default on loans given in good faith. Even church leaders are viewed with suspicion due to high-profile figures that have been exposed as "living a lie."

Few things erode the essential foundation of trust in a relationship as quickly as broken promises and exposed falsehoods—whether big or small. Commitments are often sacrificed on the altar of convenience, especially when the price tag of keeping one's word demands more than a person is willing to pay. Integrity involves thoughtful and enduring commitment—in marriage, parenting, friendships, work, and ministry.

Extensive research recently published in the *Canadian Journal of Behavioural Science* provided interesting data.[2] Of the 257 individuals in the study, about *one-third* of participants told three to seven lies a week. The majority, however, claimed to tell two or fewer lies a week. In biblical terms, one lie a week would be too many. The research indicated a variety of reasons people lie:

1. To avoid being judged or feeling shame
2. With the aim of avoiding punishment
3. To protect themselves from retaliation
4. For no "good reason" (e.g., compulsive lying)
5. To present themselves in a positive way and impress others
6. To obtain rewards
7. Due to carelessness and impulsiveness
8. To experience pleasure from deceiving others
9. With the aim of keeping personal information secret

10. For prosocial reasons—to make others (and oneself) happy, such as telling children that Santa Claus is real
11. For altruistic reasons—to protect others from harm[3]

We all can find a few motivations that justify our tendency to "stretch the truth." Yes, there are examples in Scripture of people lying for altruistic reasons.[4] Yet the paramount truth of Scripture is that untruth is precarious.

> Lying lips are an abomination to the LORD, but those who deal faithfully are His delight. (Prov. 12:22)

> Therefore, laying aside falsehood, speak truth each one of you with his neighbor, for we are members of one another. (Eph. 4:25)

> Do not lie to one another, since you laid aside the old self with its evil practices. (Col. 3:9)

Operating behind all the insincere commitments and false promises is one who wants to disrupt your life and relationships. Satan is always eager to help you slide away on a slippery slope of deception and relational destruction. Jesus exposed him with these words: "He was a murderer from the beginning, and does not stand in the truth because there is no truth in him. Whenever he speaks a lie, he speaks from his own nature, for he is a liar and the father of lies" (John 8:44).

Of course, the power to overcome all forms of fakery and our proneness to lie is found in the gospel of Christ. Jesus is "the way, and the truth, and the life" (John 14:6). Because of the power of His saving grace and empowering life, we live in His promise: "You will know the truth, and the truth will make you free" (John 8:32).

Commitment Aversion

Psalm 15:4 unpacks the firm reality of truthful living, starting with "he swears to his own hurt." In Hebrew, the word "swear" draws from the everyday imagery of the language. It literally means to "seven" oneself. It is the idea of a sevenfold strand. You could illustrate this by taking seven strands of rope, maybe even kite string, and tying them tightly around your hands, clasped together. Even the strongest offensive lineman for the Dallas Cowboys would need help to break this restriction. This is a commitment that is firm, unbreakable, and sincere.

Today, individuals with "commitment aversion" populate our communities, workplaces, churches, and families. They struggle to go "all in"—whether it involves choosing a college, committing to marriage, having children, a more demanding job promotion, signing a lease, serving in the church, making a significant purchase, or deciding on the paint color in the living room. Whether it is an irrational fear or severe anxiety, they just can't "seven" themselves.

The gospel's transforming power can bring healing and credibility to our commitments. Our identity, trust, and assurance become rooted in the person and promises of Christ. Our confidence is in His present and future leadership, not our past confusion. Our decisions are rooted in His wisdom. Our hope remains secure because His power strengthens us in fulfilling life's commitments.

To Swear or Not to Swear

So, what guidance can we find when we lean toward "sevening" ourselves? You may recall that Ecclesiastes 5:1–7 tells us to guard our steps and avoid impulsivity of any kind when making commitments, especially to God.

When you make a vow to God, do not be late in paying it; for He takes no delight in fools. Pay what you vow! It is

better that you should not vow than that you should vow
and not pay. Do not let your speech cause you to sin and do
not say in the presence of the messenger of God that it was a
mistake. Why should God be angry on account of your voice
and destroy the work of your hands? For in many dreams and
in many words there is emptiness. Rather, fear God. (vv. 4–7)

So, in reality, our commitments are ultimately to an audience of
One. We may tell a friend that we will help them move. We might
promise to babysit next Thursday night. We might commit to serving weekly in the children's ministry at church. But ultimately, our
commitment is made from a sincere reverence for an all-knowing,
unchanging God of truth.

In Jesus' day, the religious culture had become so diluted that
one's word did not mean much. One commentator notes that there
was significant "concern about the devaluation of oaths because of
their indiscriminate use and the tendency to try to avoid fulfilling
them by swearing by 'less sacred' things."[5]

The Lord laid it out this way:

"Again, you have heard that the ancients were told, 'You shall
not make false vows, but shall fulfill your vows to the Lord.'
But I say to you, make no oath at all, either by heaven, for it
is the throne of God, or by the earth, for it is the footstool of
His feet, or by Jerusalem, for it is the city of the great King.
Nor shall you make an oath by your head, for you cannot
make one hair white or black. But let your statement be, 'Yes,
yes' or 'No, no'; anything beyond these is of evil."
(Matt. 5:33–37)

In his inspired letter, James reiterated the same truth, "But above
all, my brethren, do not swear, either by heaven or by earth or with

any other oath; but your yes is to be yes, and your no, no, so that you may not fall under judgment" (James 5:12).

So our commitments need to be clear and sincere. In essence, we say what we mean and mean what we say. We simply give our word with full intention to keep our word because relationships matter. Integrity matters. The reputation of a never-shaken life matters.

Pain Avoidance

Note the challenge we all face in our commitments. "He swears *to his own hurt*." Disciples of Christ are cautioned to "count the cost" of our decisions before we make them. "For which of you, desiring to build a tower, does not first sit down and count the cost, whether he has enough to complete it?" (Luke 14:28 ESV). In the broader context of Luke 14 (vv. 25–33), Jesus makes it clear that it is costly to follow Him as a true disciple.

Still, many of our legitimate commitments come with a price tag we did not (and often cannot) anticipate in advance. That's when a never-shaken Christ follower presses into the reality of this truth by God's grace.

> WE SIMPLY GIVE OUR WORD WITH FULL INTENTION TO KEEP OUR WORD BECAUSE RELATIONSHIPS MATTER. INTEGRITY MATTERS. THE REPUTATION OF A NEVER-SHAKEN LIFE MATTERS.

Marriage is costly. It involves suffering. I'm not trying to throw your spouse under the bus here, but marriage requires sacrifice, mutual submission, honesty to confront my weaknesses, and a humble willingness to change.

Parenting is a whole new level of discomfort for the self-preserving soul. Each child has unique personalities, demands, and needs that easily consume every available ounce of energy, trumping the personal needs of Mom or Dad.

Work is, well, *work*. Work is not always "fun." It is commonly difficult, demanding, and tiring. Indeed, there are aspects of fulfillment, but the hidden price tag unfolds over long years of sustained effort.

Students also feel the stress that comes with a commitment to education. School can be tiresome. The semester becomes fatiguing. A loan can be hard to repay.

The point is that our commitments can prove problematic. Our decisions can lead through some rugged terrain. Things turn out contrary to our gratification. Kept promises seem inconvenient. Still, the never-shaken disciple can be counted on to keep their word and finish what they start.

Convenient Impulsiveness

Impulsive people can make insincere commitments. The emotion of the moment can prompt a promise not kept. People pleasers feel burdened to say yes when they should say no. The pressure to conform to the expectations or environment around you can lead to caving in. We've all been there once—or a hundred times.

Psalm 15:4 calls us to clear commitment. Then comes the "hurt" factor of keeping that commitment. The final aspect of this integrity issue states that "he . . . does not change." Or, as the NIV states, this person "does not change their mind."

The Hebrew word for "change" can mean to exchange or even to barter for food. If you've traveled internationally and visited open markets, you know how this might look. I've done it in Mexico, Israel, and other countries. We barter to get to the bottom line because we suspect the seller will change their mind.

You can picture it in our daily relationships. "Well, I know I said I would help you all day. How about just four hours? How about two hours? How about I pray for you? I've had some other stuff come up. Sorry." In a sense, we barter. The bottom line is wiggly. The commitment needs to be clarified. The outcome is questionable. The words of James are applicable here: "Your yes is to be yes, and your no, no, so that you may not fall under judgment" (James 5:12).

An Honorable Option

So, you may ask: "Is there no grace for my broken word?" Both the Old and New Testaments provide some wisdom. Proverbs 6:1–5 advises:

> My son, if you have become surety for your neighbor, have given a pledge for a stranger, if you have been snared with the words of your mouth, have been caught with the words of your mouth, do this then, my son, and deliver yourself; since you have come into the hand of your neighbor, go, humble yourself, and importune your neighbor. Give no sleep to your eyes, nor slumber to your eyelids; deliver yourself like a gazelle from the hunter's hand and like a bird from the hand of the fowler.

So, in the possibility of appealing to a merciful and sympathetic neighbor, we can humble ourselves, admit our folly, and hope for forgiveness. In this approach, we must see the seriousness of our commitment and the gravity of what it means to break our word. We do not just cast off our fickleness but genuinely appeal for reprieve—and it must be for good reasons.

Deuteronomy 23:21–23 underscores the weightiness of making and keeping our word:

> "When you make a vow to the LORD your God, you shall not delay to pay it, for it would be sin in you, and the LORD your God will surely require it of you. However, if you refrain from vowing, it would not be sin in you. You shall be careful to perform what goes out from your lips, just as you

have voluntarily vowed to the LORD your God, what you have promised."

God expects us to measure our commitments carefully. In worship, relationships, and all of life, it is better not to make a promise rather than make and break it, since breaking our commitment is a sin. In the Old Testament, this required atonement through sacrifice.

> PSALM 15 DRAWS A DIRECT LINE FROM SOMEONE WHO KEEPS THEIR WORD TO GOD'S PROMISE FOR AN UNSHAKEN LIFE.

Because of the wonder of the gospel, the atonement for all of our sin has been paid by Christ. He made the sacrifice on the cross. Now, we come to His throne of grace "so that we may receive mercy and find grace to help in time of need" (Heb. 4:16). First John 1:9 promises, "If we confess our sins, He is faithful and righteous to forgive us our sins and to cleanse us from all unrighteousness."

So we must believe that breaking our word is not just a casual mess. It is sin. Thankfully, there is a Redeemer. We have a Restorer of the relationships damaged by insincerity. We have the Spirit of truth indwelling converted hearts. He empowers us to know, commit to, and keep the truth.

Our Word, Our Bond

When keeping our word hurts us, we need to remember that breaking our word will often hurt others even more. A broken marriage vow can devastate your children. A fickle day at work can damage your boss or company. A lazy attitude toward serving at the church can hurt the work of the gospel. But, most of all, compromised commitments throw shade on the name and reputation of Christ in this world. If unbelieving friends can't trust us, they may conclude that they cannot trust the gospel that we claim to trust.

Psalm 15 draws a direct line from someone who keeps their word to God's promise for an unshaken life. A Psalm 15 God follower embodies stability and demonstrates reliability. As a result, this person enjoys integrity and profound satisfaction in relationships.

A Promise Kept Through Peril

The Oscar-winning film *1917* recounts the events of World War I in April 1917. British troops were preparing a major offensive against the German troops that had strategically arranged a setup for the Brits. Aerial reconnaissance had discovered the ploy. Phone lines to the battlefront were cut.

Two young soldiers, Will Schofield and Tom Blake, accepted a dangerous assignment to deliver an essential message to the 2nd Battalion with a directive to abort the attack. Blake's brother, Joseph, was part of that battalion. The mission required the two young soldiers to traverse treacherous territory on foot to deliver the urgent order by dawn. If they succeeded, they could save the lives of 1,600 soldiers.

Watching the film, I felt the constant suspense of wondering if Schofield and Blake would survive the barrage of bombs and bullets to fulfill their promise. Time was their enemy. Would they lose heart and abort the struggle?

The pair battled serious injury and unpredictable perils. They had countless reasons to turn back. (Spoiler alert if you've not seen the movie.) Tragically, Blake was stabbed to death while trying to help an enemy pilot whose plane had been shot down. As Schofield comforted his dying companion, he took Blake's rings and dog tags, promising to deliver them to his brother, Joseph. He pledged to write to Blake's mother recounting his bravery and resolve. As the story unfolds, Schofield is shot and delayed by various perils. He eventually sprints across an open battlefield to reach the officer in charge—just in time to avert the tragedy.

The story of two young soldiers who "swore to their own hurt" at great cost and without wavering illustrates the nobility and impact of keeping promises. It's the Psalm 15 way. It is the way of Christ, to whom we look and on whose grace we depend. Keeping our word, we can "run with endurance the race that is set before us, fixing our eyes on Jesus, the author and perfecter of faith, who for the joy set before Him endured the cross, despising the shame, and has sat down at the right hand of the throne of God" (Heb. 12:1–2).

Jesus, our ultimate Promise Keeper, has transformed countless lives. He endured. He knew it was worth it. He lives in and through you to do the same until you join Him in your eternal reward for a never-shaken life.

Never Shaken Application

- Has anyone ever made a clear commitment to you and not kept their word? How did this affect the relationship? Were there negative consequences for you? If so, what were they, and how did you handle it?
- Have you ever made a commitment to another person only to break your word? What was the situation? Were you able to make things right? What was the outcome?
- As you think about the commitment you need to keep in specific relationships, how will the principle of this chapter help you? Pray now for the grace to make these applications in order to cultivate honorable and healthy relationships.

Chapter 11

WHY MONEY MATTERS

He does not put out his money at interest,
Nor does he take a bribe against the innocent.

PSALM **15:5**

Money and things are a big part of life, and therefore God intends
them to be a big part of worship—since all of life is to be worship.
So the way you worship with your money and your possessions
is to get them and use them and lose them in a way that shows how
much you treasure God—not money.

JOHN **P**IPER

once heard a fictitious story of a love-struck young man. Let's call
him Jason. He was proposing to his girlfriend, Susan. As they sat together enjoying a quiet moment, he mustered up his courage. "Susan,
I love you. I want to spend the rest of my life with you." Susan smiled
sweetly. "Now, Susan," Jason continued, "I don't have the money that
Steve Adams has. I can't buy you a new car or give you a Nordstrom
card as he could. I can't buy a new home and give you all the vaca-
tions like Steve can. But I love you with all of my heart. Will you
marry me?" Susan responded, "Well, Jason, I love you too, and thank
you for your kind proposal. But tell me more about Steve Adams."

Money exerts tremendous influence on our lives and, especially,
our relationships. People marry for money. People divorce over money.
Friendships form and fracture because of financial interests. Business
partnerships foster and falter because of fractures around money.

People will kill for money. Women will give birth to another couple's child for money. Some lie for money, and others will spill the truth for money. Some people live for money; some die for it. Personal prosperity and poverty are rooted in the reality of money. The rich and poor social dynamics are profound in this world.

> YOUR BODY'S MOST SENSITIVE NERVE MAY NOT BE YOUR FUNNY BONE. INSTEAD, IT COULD BE THE NERVE THAT CONNECTS YOUR HEART TO YOUR WALLET OR PURSE.

According to a study by Ramsey Solutions, the number one issue couples fight about is also a topic many couples avoid discussing—money. Conflicts over money are the second leading cause of divorce, behind infidelity. Results show that both high levels of debt and a lack of communication are significant causes for the stress and anxiety surrounding household finances.[1]

Your body's most sensitive nerve may not be your funny bone. Instead, it could be the nerve that connects your heart to your wallet or purse. Bring up the subject of money, and people tend to react. Indeed, we all like to hear about cash if someone's telling us how to make more of it. If we're lectured about what to do with what we think is ours, the defenses go up.

The average person can feel shaken to the core when it feels like their money is sliding away, whether by job loss, overspending, medical bills, or economic downturn. Anxiety builds. Tensions rise. Uncertainty looms. The outlook can grow very dark.

Singing About Money

David's song began with a central question in verse 1 concerning the one who truly knows God. He queried the Lord about the character of a true worshiper. Now, in what may seem a surprising turn, the Holy Spirit inspires a direct line from the soul of a true worshiper to the reality of what money reveals about the heart. No doubt, the core of a never-shaken disciple must be at peace about the paramount issue of money. The final verse of Psalm 15 states it directly, although the application may not be clear at first. "He does not put out his money at interest, nor does he take a bribe against the innocent" (Ps. 15:5).

We do not know for certain, but there is the possibility that Absalom used money to gain influence. Maybe he paid people off if only they would join his rebellious cause. Perhaps he promised them a piece of the proceeds once he came into power.

David was no stranger to wealth and power. He knew he could use money as a tool for influence—good or bad. God knows the temptation of every human when it comes to currency. He knew the musings of David's soul as he sang. So, in divine wisdom, God addresses our heart's attitude concerning money. The bottom line is that, in the outflow and income of money, we can never allow it to undermine biblical, Christ-honoring relationships. Instead, it must be an expression of our obedience to the great commandments to love the Lord our God with all our heart, soul, mind, and strength, and to love our neighbor as ourselves (Mark 12:30–31).

The Magnitude of Money

The Bible contains over two thousand verses about money, tithing, and possessions. There are twice as many verses about money as faith and prayer combined. Of Jesus' parables, sixteen out of thirty-eight in some way speak of money and possessions as illustrations of spiritual truth.[2] Richard Halverson, former chaplain of the US Senate, noted, "Money is an exact index to a man's true character. All through Scripture there is an intimate correlation between the development of a man's character and how he handles his money."[3]

Psalm 15 has carefully portrayed the character qualities of a true worshiper. In essence, we either worship our money and the things it provides or set our hearts to worship with our money and the God who provides.

> WE EITHER WORSHIP OUR MONEY AND THE THINGS IT PROVIDES OR SET OUR HEARTS TO WORSHIP WITH OUR MONEY AND THE GOD WHO PROVIDES.

Consider Jesus' warning: "No one can serve two masters; for either he will hate the one and love the other, or he will be devoted to one and despise the other. You cannot serve God and wealth" (Matt. 6:24). Money is an issue of the heart, "for where your treasure is, there your heart will be also" (Matt. 6:21).

Scripture tells us that when we trust the Lord's promise of His presence and provision, our character can authentically be free from the love of money. We can live in daily contentment because we believe His promise, "I will never desert you, nor will I ever forsake you" (Heb. 13:5). He is enough, whether in scarcity or abundance.

Why an Interest in Interest?

Why would God inspire David to write, "He does not put out his money at interest"? Today, many drive a bank-financed Honda on a bond-financed highway using Shell-credit-card-provided gas and open a charge account at Macy's so we can fill our Rocket Mortgage–financed home with installment-purchased IKEA furniture. Interest seems woven into our existence.

Interest is not wrong. It can be a helpful tool. Interest is essential in global trade and local business dealings. Yet we are warned to be wise because "the rich rules over the poor, and the borrower becomes the lender's slave" (Prov. 22:7).

Water is a good thing. We are encouraged to drink eight glasses a day. But too much water will drown a person. Fire is a good thing. It will cook your dinner and warm your house. But too much fire will burn your house down. Food is a good thing. The right amount and a proper diet will keep you healthy and well. But an overabundance of carbs and sugar will eventually make you sick and obese.

So it is with debt. Debt can be helpful or harmful. A recent report from the Federal Reserve indicated that Americans' credit card debt is rising at its fastest clip in more than twenty years. This is happening simultaneously as the Fed raises interest rates to contain inflation, putting credit card rates at 19.9 percent, their highest level in thirty years. Some have maxed out credit cards and are paying a 29.7 percent interest rate.[4] Of course, the numbers change yearly, but they remind us of the need for wisdom and discipline. The numbers also give us a glimpse into our hearts and perspectives on money.

The Hebrew word for interest (*nesek*) means "bite." It refers to taking a bite out of something or biting off something. The old-school word for a harmful use of interest is "usury." This referred to a requirement of interest that unfairly enriched the lender while unjustly harming the borrower.

A Biblical Lack of Interest

Interest was a legitimate tool of the trade for Jews engaged in business dealings with non-Jews. It was a sum paid to a creditor, in money or goods, at a fixed or accelerating percentage rate for the use of borrowed money or goods. But, in the context of Old Testament life, there is something deeper here—something beyond the numbers. Deuteronomy 23:19–20 clarifies,

> "You shall not charge interest to your countrymen: interest on money, food, or anything that may be loaned at interest. You may charge interest to a foreigner, but to your countrymen you shall not charge interest, so that the LORD your God may bless you in all that you undertake in the land which you are about to enter to possess."

Exodus 22:25 affirms, "If you lend money to My people, to the poor among you, you are not to act as a creditor to him; you shall not charge him interest."

Within the faith community of Israel, interest was taboo. When a fellow Jew was in need, it was typically due to hardship. Old Testament families never needed a loan to purchase more unnecessary goodies as advertised on QVC. They did not need extra funds to invest in the latest Bitcoin opportunity. The point of a loan was to lend a genuine helping hand in serving your brother. Thus, money was an avenue of benevolence and ministry. Exodus 23:11 reminds us that the poor were so important to God that every seventh year the Jewish people were to refrain from plowing their fields so that the poor could have the harvest. The Bible repeatedly reiterates that when you lend to the poor you lend to the Lord. If you take advantage of the poor, you displease the Lord.

FOR YOU AND ME, THE CONCERN IS NOT ABOUT CURRENT INTEREST RATES BUT THE INTERESTS OF THE HEART.

For you and me, the concern is not about current interest rates but the interests of the heart. God requires a heart that worships and serves through the use of money. Therefore, the attitude that motivates how our money goes out should demonstrate integrity and sincerity.

Greedy for Gain

The follow-up financial concern in Psalm 15:5 states: "Nor does he take a bribe against the innocent." This truth addresses how we gain income. We all know the temptation of somehow pocketing a little more cash on the side just by some subtle compromise.

Perhaps you saw the story of a seventy-year-old nun who stole over $835,000 from the Catholic school she ran in Southern California to finance her gambling habit. Violating her vow of poverty over ten years, she pocketed tuition money, fees, and charitable donations.[5] In other news, a church treasurer stole $150,000 from his Lutheran church in Pennsylvania over four years to fund his porn addiction.[6] What rarely makes the news or sends people to prison is the less bombastic ways we figure out how to get a little bit more out of the people in our circle of influence.

Psalm 15:5 refers specifically to bribery. A bribe is "money or favor given or promised in order to influence the judgment or conduct of a person in a position of trust."[7] Exodus 23:8 warns, "You shall not take a bribe, for a bribe blinds the clear-sighted and subverts the cause of the just." Proverbs 15:27 affirms, "He who profits illicitly troubles his own house, but he who hates bribes will live." So the greed of bribery clouds our judgment and undermines justice. It brings more trouble than it's worth. Just as charging interest can bite the borrower, taking a bribe can eventually bite the culpable recipient and those he loves.

A recent four-part Netflix documentary called *FIFA Uncovered* exposed a high-profile bribery scandal involving a key Qatari FIFA board official. The accusation concludes that he secretly offered $1.5 million in bribes to three FIFA voters from Africa back in 2012, effectively buying votes to assure that the 2022 World Cup would be held in the Middle East. As a result, Qatar won hosting rights for the 2022 tournament in a FIFA vote ahead of Australia, Japan, South Korea, and the USA.[8] Amid the turmoil, FIFA's longtime president Sepp Blatter abruptly announced his resignation just days after winning a fifth term as the governing body's leader.[9] As a result, controversy mired the 2022 World Cup.

What rarely makes the news is the everyday forms of "bribery" involving promises of kickbacks, an influential seat at the table, or a bigger platform if only you will pay me "X" amount up front. Among the Jews in David's day, it was never acceptable for a true worshiper. Today, all forms of bribery contradict the testimony and truth of the one who knows Christ and wants their use of money to reflect their worship.

Finding Fulfillment in Our Funding

If the chief end of man is to glorify God and enjoy Him forever (as stated by the Westminster Confession), then the chief end of money must be the same. Psalm 15:5 is best understood in this context. Usury, bribery, and all forms of greed diminish God's glory in our lives and undermine our purpose in this brief appearance on earth. So, why money after all? How do we fulfill God's purpose for our funds?

First, God has entrusted us with money to **advance His eternal purposes**. When we realize that all of our money is God's money, not ours, we want to steward what is His for His glory. When we give to the work of the gospel, whether at our church or through another biblical mission, we store up "treasures in heaven, where neither moth nor rust destroys, and where thieves do not break in or steal" (Matt. 6:20).

Money also serves the convenient purpose of **meeting our basic needs** in this earthly life. The first biblical mention of money is found in Genesis 17:12. God spoke to Abraham about purchasing and circumcising foreign workers to help with his many household needs. God's blessing brought wealth to Abraham, and money was a tool for managing that abundance. Jesus sent the disciples to buy food using their ministry treasury because He knew they needed to eat to live and conduct the work of the ministry (John 4:8).

The apostle Paul spoke of our basic requirements when he wrote, "My God will supply all your needs according to His riches in glory in Christ Jesus" (Phil. 4:19). Needs are different from "wants." This is where many of us get tripped up today. Our information society bombards us with countless forms of advertising. Advertising tends to produce discontent. It caters mainly to our wants, not our needs. If advertising did not exist, most of us would only own half the clothes in our closets and much less of the junk that fills our garages. Advertising reminds us that if we don't buy something new, we're not going to be happy or fulfilled.

Paul taught otherwise. His words may be familiar to us, but we cannot let familiarity breed complacency.

> But godliness actually is a means of great gain when accompanied by contentment. For we have brought nothing into the world, so we cannot take anything out of it either. If we have food and covering, with these we shall be content. But those who want to get rich fall into temptation and a snare and many foolish and harmful desires which plunge men into ruin and destruction. For the love of money is a root of all sorts of evil, and some by longing for it have wandered away from the faith and pierced themselves with many griefs. (1 Tim. 6:6–10)

A third reason we have been entrusted with money is to **minister to others**. As we steward our personal currency, our funds must be thoroughfares, not cul-de-sacs. The danger of "more" is that we might hoard larger and larger slices of the prosperity pie for ourselves. We are tempted to look at the increased amounts we give away rather than evaluate the percentage of our assets that are generously passed on. God sees our stewardship not in terms of the quantity but in the growing degree of sacrifice.

The gospel commends the Good Samaritan who was not too busy with his own business to notice, care, and sacrifice for a needy man. The letter from James revisits the familiar biblical theme that true religion cares for the penniless widow and the fatherless orphan (James 1:27). James goes on to say, "If a brother or sister is without clothing and in need of daily food, and one of you says to them, 'Go in peace, be warmed and be filled,' and yet you do not

> THE DANGER OF "MORE" IS THAT WE MIGHT HOARD LARGER AND LARGER SLICES OF THE PROSPERITY PIE FOR OURSELVES.

give them what is necessary for their body, what use is that?" (James 2:15–16). Similarly, the apostle John admonishes, "But whoever has the world's goods, and sees his brother in need and closes his heart against him, how does the love of God abide in him? Little children, let us not love with word or with tongue, but in deed and truth" (1 John 3:17–18). First Timothy 6:17–19 instructs those who are "rich in this present world" (which would be most Americans compared to the rest of the world) "to do good, to be rich in good works, to be generous and ready to share, storing up for themselves the treasure of a good foundation for the future, so that they may take hold of that which is life indeed."

Money can certainly be an avenue that **tests our hearts**. Psalm 15 is clear by including this in the description of a never-shaken life. How we handle money reveals the genuineness of our worship and the integrity of our relationships.

How Greed Can Kill

A legendary account of how Eskimos take care of the problem of predatory wolves that ravage their livestock illustrates the temptation of our financial foolishness.

> First, the Eskimo coats his knife blade with animal blood and allows it to freeze. Then he adds another layer of blood, and another, until the blade is completely concealed by frozen blood. Next, the hunter fixes his knife in the ground with the blade up. When a wolf follows his sensitive nose to the source of the scent and discovers the bait, he licks it, tasting the fresh frozen blood. He begins to lick faster, more and more vigorously, lapping the blade until the keen edge is bare. Feverishly now, harder and harder the wolf licks the blade in the arctic night.
>
> So great becomes his craving for blood that the wolf does

not notice the razor-sharp sting of the naked blade on his own tongue, nor does he recognize the instant at which his insatiable thirst is being satisfied by his OWN warm blood. His carnivorous appetite just craves more—until the dawn finds him dead in the snow![10]

The message for us all is clear: Be careful what you crave. Think *relationships* over *resources*. Remind yourself regularly that the biblical management of money and a rejection of the dangerous temptations toward "more" are core to a never-shaken life in a world that is sliding away in greed.

Never Shaken Application

- Have you ever been tempted to get more money in a way that could hurt other people? If so, what was it, and how did you resolve the situation?
- As you consider God's purposes for your money as noted in this chapter, how do you feel you need to align your budget to more intentionally fulfill these purposes? What practical steps do you need to take this week toward that objective?
- As you look at your giving patterns, is there evidence that you are growing in the grace of generosity? How is this evident? What percentage of your income did you pass on to God's work last year? Did that percentage increase this year, and if so, by what degree? (See Paul's comment on giving in 2 Corinthians 8:7.)

THE PROMISING PLAYLIST
OF THE HEART

He who does these things will never be shaken.

PSALM 15:5

A heart set on God will be preserved through all loss,
all devastation, and will be delivered in the eternal,
loving embrace of the Father.

DAVE KEESLING

The story is told that after World War I, Lawrence of Arabia visited Paris. He was accompanied by friends who had never been outside the desert. Lawrence showed them the City of Lights, but he was amused to find them most fascinated by the faucets in their rooms. They constantly turned them on and off, marveling at the instant supply of water. While packing to leave, Lawrence found them in the bathroom trying to detach the faucets. "It's very dry in Arabia," they explained. "What we need are faucets."[1]

This world of ours is very dry. Integrity is evaporating like sprinkler overspray on a Phoenix sidewalk in August. Our human sense of certainty is sliding away like a mirage in the Mojave Desert. Psalm 15 might be seen as a divine "faucet," delivering refreshment and life-giving truth for hearts thirsting for security and strength. As I have memorized these verses and taught from this inspired song, my mind has often been renewed and my focus reset on the principles of integrity in my personal life, my relationships, and my money.

But as we conclude our journey together, we cannot just walk away with the faucet. We must realize that God looks at the heart. The heart that genuinely knows God, through the finished work of Christ, experiences the "water" of a never-shaken earthly experience.

The faucet is a wonderful provider of essential guidance. But we must have the water. Speaking of His gospel, Jesus said, "Whoever drinks of the water that I will give him shall never thirst; but the water that I will give him will become in him a well of water springing up to eternal life" (John 4:14).

> **THE WORST OF TIMES ARE OFTEN THE BEST OF TIMES, EVEN THOUGH THEY DO NOT FEEL LIKE IT AT THE TIME.**

The apostle Paul penned these encouraging words, "Therefore we do not lose heart, but though our outer man is decaying, yet our inner man is being renewed day by day" (2 Cor. 4:16). What I need every day is a renewal of soul, rooted in the realities of a never-shaken life. I have declared hundreds of times that the hardest thing about the Christian life is that it is so daily. I also believe that the worst of times are often the best of times, even though they do not feel like it at the time.

Every day of this life, and especially in our most excruciating moments, our parched souls need a renewal that can only come from the living water of Jesus Christ. He imparts grace and strength to turn our mourning into dancing. We must choose it daily.

David's Playlist of the Soul

Most modern-day music lovers have a digital playlist or two (or ten). I currently have seventeen on my iPhone. I have specific worship playlists on the themes of the goodness of God, the hope of heaven, and prayer. I have created a list of my favorite contemporary Christian songs from specific years. I have an upbeat playlist to enliven my day and a collection of quiet instrumental music that I play in the background when reading or working. Frequently, I even borrow playlists created by others on Apple Music when they fit the mood of the moment.

We could say that David had a playlist called "Absalom's Rebellion, My Reassurance." Perhaps "Confidence in Crisis." Maybe a simple title like "Never Shaken." The uniting promise interwoven through every song was "he who does these things will never be shaken" (Ps. 15:5).

Various commentators have tagged other psalms as composed while David was in exile. We noted some in chapter 2. In the short period of time that David was surviving his onslaught of banishment, he was still thriving. The water of his soul was flowing with trust in his ever-living God. So for some fortified reassurance, let's consider critical lines from David's songs that can provide a life-giving flow of promise for our never-shaken life.

As we conclude, let's sing our way with David through these essential reassurances. Imagine again the pain and betrayal he was navigating as his notes formed into melodies. Consider the trust God was rebirthing in him. His familiar world had slid away—but still, he sang. His confident faith echoed across the Middle Eastern plains as he trusted his Lord through the most harrowing moments. Drink deeply as you experience that same truth and similar trust.

We Sing Because . . .

Because the strength and security of God is greater than the opinions and opposition of the crowd, we can trust the Lord for confidence and hope. "Many are saying of my soul, 'There is no deliverance for him in God.' But You, O LORD, are a shield about me, my glory, and the One who lifts my head" (Ps. 3:2–3).

Because God alone can provide real peace and safety, we can sing at the end of each day, "In peace I will both lie down and sleep, for You alone, O LORD, make me to dwell in safety" (Ps. 4:8).

Because He is the ultimate refuge and shelter, we can joyfully sing of our love for His great name, knowing that His favor on our life is the impenetrable shield. "But let all who take refuge in You be glad, let them ever sing for joy; and may You shelter them, that those who love Your name may exult in You. For it is You who blesses the righteous man, O LORD, You surround him with favor as with a shield" (Ps. 5:11–12).

Because He graciously shapes and strengthens our hearts to live with integrity, we know our feet can remain firm. For this, we sing blessings to Him in the gathering of His people. "But as for me, I shall walk in my integrity; redeem me, and be gracious to me. My foot stands on a level place; in the congregations I shall bless the LORD" (Ps. 26:11–12).

Because He is light and salvation, we can sing of His sure defense of our life, knowing that He is all-powerful to destroy a host of adversaries and enemies. Our song of confidence overshadows all fear. "The LORD is my light and my salvation; whom shall I fear? The LORD is the defense of my life; whom shall I dread? When evildoers came upon me to devour my flesh, my adversaries and my enemies, they stumbled and fell. Though a host encamp against me, my heart will not fear; though war arise against me, in spite of this I shall be confident" (Ps. 27:1–3).

Because the power of His presence in us is greater than any forces in this world, we sing praises to the Lord. Even in the days of severe trouble, He delivers us. He graciously answers our cries, assuring us that He is indeed the solid rock on which we stand. "For in the day of trouble He will conceal me in His tabernacle; in the secret place of His tent He will hide me; He will lift me up on a rock. And now my head will be lifted up above my enemies around me, and I will offer in His tent sacrifices with shouts of joy; I will sing, yes, I will sing praises to the LORD. Hear, O LORD, when I cry with my voice, and be gracious to me and answer me" (Ps. 27:5–7).

Because we have real hope in the help of His presence and His unfailing lovingkindness, we can fight through our questions and despair, knowing that our song of praise will rise from the dark seasons of life. "Why are you in despair, O my soul? And why have you become disturbed within me? Hope in God, for I shall again praise Him for the help of His presence. . . . The LORD will command His lovingkindness in the daytime; and His song will be with me in the night, a prayer to the God of my life" (Ps. 42:5, 8).

Because He redeems us in His peace from our battles and adversaries, we lift a song to cast our burden on Him with the confidence that we will never be shaken. He will sustain us as He, at the same time, defeats our enemies. In song, we declare our trust. "He will redeem my soul in peace from the battle which is against me, for they are many who strive with me. . . . Cast your burden upon the LORD and He will sustain you; He will never allow the righteous to be shaken. But You, O God, will bring them down to the pit of destruction; men of bloodshed and deceit will not live out half their days. But I will trust in You" (Ps. 55:18, 22–23).

Because all other sources of security and strength ultimately fail and disappoint, we sing of the salvation that only He provides. We rest on our Rock—unshaken. We pause silently to contemplate this assurance, waiting on Him alone. "My soul waits in silence for God only; from Him is my salvation. He only is my rock and my salvation, my stronghold; I shall not be greatly shaken" (Ps. 62:1–2).

Because when we cling to Him, He upholds us. We sing joyfully of His help in the shadow of His wings. We are confident that He will defeat every enemy that seeks to destroy us. "For You have been my help, and in the shadow of Your wings I sing for joy. My soul clings to You; Your right hand upholds me. But those who seek my life to destroy it, will go into the depths of the earth" (Ps. 63:7–9).

Because He gives what is good as we walk uprightly, we declare

His grace and glory in song. As our sun and shield, we know the profound blessing of trusting in Him. "For the LORD God is a sun and shield; the LORD gives grace and glory; no good thing does He withhold from those who walk uprightly. O LORD of hosts, how blessed is the man who trusts in You!" (Ps. 84:11–12).

Psalm 23 might have also emerged from David's soul during a season of devastating rejection. Perhaps the most well-known song in human history flowed from a moment of deep pain but deeper trust. Imagine all that had slid away from David. Consider the greater reality of a tender, divine Shepherd, caring once again for the shepherd boy who became a king, and, now, an exile in his own land. Imagine the infusion of care, peace, assurance, and hope that inspires the life-changing refrains.

REST IN HIM DURING YOUR PRESENT MOMENT OF UNCERTAINTY. BELIEVE HIS PROMISE FOR ALL THAT LIES AHEAD—UNPREDICTABLE AS IT MAY SEEM.

Because the Lord is your shepherd, you can remain unshaken. Like David, trust Him for all that has been taken away in recent years. Rest in Him during your present moment of uncertainty. Believe His promise for all that lies ahead—unpredictable as it may seem.

Believe that Yahweh, who has invited you into the most profound, most fulfilling intimacy conceivable, will faithfully shape the character of Christ in you. He will bring healing and health to your relationships in every dimension.

Yes, sing the familiar tune now.

The LORD is my shepherd, I shall not want. He makes me lie down in green pastures; He leads me beside quiet waters. He restores my soul; He guides me in the paths of righteousness for His name's sake. Even though I walk through the valley of the shadow of death, I fear no evil, for You are with me; Your rod and Your staff, they comfort me. You prepare a table before me in the presence of my enemies; You have anointed my head with oil; my cup overflows. Surely goodness and lovingkindness will follow me all the days of my life, and I will dwell in the house of the LORD forever. (Ps. 23)

When your world falls apart, *you* do not have to. Your well-being and confidence are not based on circumstances, but rather on God, who rules over the circumstances. So, start your own Psalm 15 playlist and sing with David. Drink deeply as you trust the person and provision of the indwelling Christ. Then, when the world is sliding away, raise your voice confidently. Plant your feet firmly. Surrender your heart in trust. Live in the power of the integrity of Jesus.

You will never be shaken.

Never Shaken Application

- How are you prone to focus on the "faucets" of your life rather than the living water of Jesus? What are your common "faucets"? How will you choose to change your focus to trust more fully in the life of Jesus?
- As you review the various excerpts from the Psalms that may have been written during this difficult season in David's life, which one speaks most relevantly to your heart right now? Turn to the entire psalm and read it with this possible context in mind: What is your primary takeaway for today?
- Finally, read Psalm 15 again, considering all it reveals about the heart. What kind of heart transformation will you trust the Lord to conduct in the coming days? Surrender anew to His power and look for the evidence of this growth over the next few weeks.

SALVATION: THE BEGINNING PLACE FOR A NEVER-SHAKEN LIFE

Salvation is deliverance. All the world religions teach that we need to be delivered, but each has a different understanding of what we need to be delivered from, why we need to be delivered, and how that deliverance can be received or achieved. The Bible makes it abundantly clear, however, that there is only one plan of salvation.

The most important thing to understand about the plan of salvation is that it is God's plan, not humanity's. Humanity's plan of salvation is about observing religious rituals, obeying certain commands, or achieving certain levels of spiritual enlightenment. But none of these things is part of God's plan of salvation.

God's Plan of Salvation – The Why

In God's salvation plan, we must first understand why we need salvation. Simply put, we need to be saved because we have sinned. The Bible declares that everyone has sinned (Eccl. 7:20; Rom. 3:10, 23; 1 John 1:8). Sin is rebellion against God. We all choose to do wrong. Sin harms others, damages us, and, most importantly, dishonors God. The Bible also teaches that because God is holy and just, He cannot allow sin to go unpunished. The punishment for sin is death (Rom. 6:23) and eternal separation from God (Rev. 20:11–15).

Without God's plan of salvation, eternal death is the destiny of every human being.

God's Plan of Salvation — The What

In God's plan of salvation, God Himself is the only one who can provide for our salvation. We are utterly unable to save ourselves because of our sin and its consequences. God became a human being in the person of Jesus Christ (John 1:1, 14). Jesus lived a sinless life (2 Cor. 5:21; Heb. 4:15; 1 John 3:5) and offered Himself as a perfect sacrifice on our behalf (1 Cor. 15:3; Col. 1:22; Heb. 10:10). Since Jesus is God, His death was of infinite and eternal value. The death of Jesus Christ on the cross fully paid for the sins of the entire world (1 John 2:2). His resurrection from the dead demonstrated that His sacrifice was indeed sufficient and that salvation is now available.

God's Plan of Salvation — The How

The Bible invites those desiring salvation to a decision of repentance and faith. The short biblical definition of repentance is "a change of mind that results in a change of action." The book of Acts especially focuses on repentance regarding salvation (Acts 2:38; 3:19; 11:18; 17:30; 20:21; 26:20). To repent concerning salvation is to change your mind regarding sin and Jesus Christ. In Peter's sermon on the day of Pentecost (Acts 2), he concludes with a call for the people to repent (Acts 2:38).

Repentance involves recognizing that you have thought wrongly in the past and determining to think rightly in the future. There is a change of disposition and a new way of thinking about God, sin, holiness, and doing God's will. True repentance is prompted by "godly sorrow," and it "leads to salvation" (2 Cor. 7:10 NIV).

In Acts 16:31, a man asked the apostle Paul how to be saved. Paul responded, "Believe in the Lord Jesus, and you will be saved." The way to follow God's plan of salvation is to believe (John 3:16; Eph. 2:8–9). God has provided for our salvation through Jesus Christ.

Repentance and faith can be understood as two sides of the same coin. It is only possible to place your faith in Jesus Christ as Savior by first changing your mind about your sin and about who Jesus is and what He has done. Whether it is repentance from willful rejection or ignorance or disinterest, it is a change of mind. Biblical repentance, in relation to salvation, is changing your mind from rejection of Christ to faith in Christ.

Saving faith is fully trusting in Jesus alone as Savior (John 1:12; 14:6; Acts 4:12). That is God's plan of salvation. A person who has truly repented of sin and exercised faith in Christ will give evidence of a changed life (2 Cor. 5:17; Gal. 5:19–23; James 2:14–26).

God's Plan of Salvation – Life's Greatest Decision

If you are ready to follow God's plan of salvation, place your faith in Jesus as your Savior. Change your mind from embracing sin and rejecting God to rejecting sin and embracing God through Jesus Christ. Fully trust in the sacrifice of Jesus as the perfect and complete payment for your sins.

As God's grace calls you to this, His Word promises that you will be saved and your sins will be forgiven. God will transform your heart and reside in you by the indwelling Holy Spirit. You will have His presence and power so that you will desire to do His will, with supernatural enabling to accomplish it (Phil. 4:13). You will receive eternal life (John 10:28; 17:3). There is no more important decision. Place your faith in Jesus Christ as your Savior and Lord today!

PSALM 3
A Prayer Guide

S trategic Renewal has produced a valuable resource, *Praying the Psalms*. This tool provides a brief commentary on each of the 150 psalms accompanied by a practical prayer guide based on the model prayer that Jesus commanded for His disciples (Matt. 6:9–13). Because of the relevance of Psalm 3 to this moment of Absalom's rebellion, we have included this excerpt from *Praying the Psalms* here. For information on the entire five-volume set, go to store.strategic renewal.com/products/praying-the-psalms-full-set-vol-1-5.

SUMMARY:

While he deals with the rebellion of his son Absalom, David is encouraged by God's protection. Clearly linked to a historical event, Psalm 3 is one of fourteen others connected to a significant event in David's life. Second Samuel 15:13ff records a detailed look at David fleeing his rebellious and vengeful son.

This psalm has a simple outline, with each point containing two verses:

1. Complaint (vv. 1–2): He listens to the wrong voice and wonders, does God care?
2. Confidence (vv. 3–4): He is refreshed in the knowledge of answered prayer.
3. Cover (vv. 5–6): He sings of safety amid danger.
4. Consolation (vv. 7–8): He strengthens himself in the Lord.

David begins with a passionate expression of grief over his son's rebellion and disloyalty. Unfortunately, we all understand the pain of someone being disloyal. The experience of betrayal is always a test. Will we lose heart? Will we push on?

David's enemies had even questioned his faith and his God. That being said, with a heart full of pain, mingled with confidence, David looks up (v. 3). He has absolute assurance in the ability of a sovereign God to provide and protect. His confidence rested in the very nature of God—He is a "shield about me," David says. God's imminent protection is just one of the many praiseworthy attributes we see in this psalm that can cause our hearts to rejoice as we look up to Him!

Despite David's weary heart, he worships God. Immediately his focus is transferred from his detractors to his glorious redeemer (v. 4). Rather than relying on himself, David finds consolation and life-giving refreshment in God (v. 5). David's request in verse 7 is urgent and compelling: "Arise, O LORD; save me, O my God."

David's confidence is so strong that he is confident his enemies will run away. Why? Because victory is a done deal! We may have this same confidence as we navigate life. As the apostle Paul reminds believers in Romans 8:37, "We are more than conquerors" (ESV). It is enough for the Lord to "stand up," and all will be well. The psalm concludes with a glorious, triumphant note of praise (v. 8). Let us praise Him. Victory in our journey belongs to the Lord.

PRAYER GUIDE:

REVERENCE – Identify and celebrate God's praiseworthy attributes (Our Father who is in heaven, hallowed be Your name.)

- Our God is always present in our difficulties (v. 1)
- He is a shield/protector during trouble (v. 3)
- We glory in Him who lifts our head / gives us hope (v. 3)
- He is holy, and He hears and answers our cries for help (v. 4)
- He sustains us and gives us rest (v. 5)

- He dispels our fears and saves/delivers us from our enemies (vv. 6–7)
- He is the God of salvation and source of blessing for His people (vv. 8–9)

Prayer Prompts:

- Even though I am facing . . . [opposition], I praise You that You are my shield.
- Thank You that You lifted my head and gave me hope when . . .
- Thank You that You have blessed me already with . . .

RESPONSE – Surrender to Him and His ways
(Your kingdom come. Your will be done, on earth as it is in heaven.)

- I confess that I have listened to doubts and accusations about . . . I surrender these and look to You alone.
- I surrender my fears about . . . trusting You to deliver me.

REQUESTS – Ask the Spirit to guide your prayer over concerns, resources, and relationships
(Give us this day our daily bread. And forgive us our debts, as we also have forgiven our debtors.)

- I trust You to be my shield today as I encounter . . .
- Because You are my sustainer, I will not be afraid of . . .
- Help [name] to glory in You today, finding hope and deliverance in You.
- Because You are a God who blesses Your people, I am asking You to bless [name].

READINESS – Encouragement and strength for spiritual battle
(And do not lead us into temptation, but deliver us from evil.)

- "Today, I trust You to save me from the enemies of . . ."

Salvation belongs to you!

PSALM 15
A Prayer Guide

(Adapted from *Praying the Psalms*, published by Strategic Renewal)

SUMMARY:

David asks the question. God gives the answer. Speaking on behalf of himself and all God seekers, King David wants to know, *Who can live in God's presence?*

God responds by describing the character traits of the person who dwells with God. Entrance into His abode is granted to the man or woman who walks right and talks right. They love right. They hate wrong. They live faultless before both God and their fellow man.

Who can satisfy these righteous requirements? No one that I know of, and neither does David. In another place he confesses, "I was brought forth in iniquity, and in sin my mother conceived me" (Ps. 51:5). No one lives like Psalm 15 requires, not fully.

But wait a minute. There was One who lived like the person described in verses 2–5. God said of Him, "This is my Beloved Son in whom I am well-pleased" (Matt. 3:17). Pontius Pilate said, "I find no guilt in Him." (John 18:38). Even an evil spirit said, "I know who You are—the Holy One of God!" (Mark 1:24). The Man Jesus Christ was perfect, blameless and without sin.

It is a good and godly desire to seek to dwell in God's presence, but there is one great obstacle that we all face: God is holy, and we are not. Our sin has separated us from God. The door into His presence is closed. We need an Advocate. Someone with access. Someone who will speak on our behalf. Jesus has opened the way for us.

It matters Who you know.

PRAYER GUIDE:

REVERENCE – Identify and celebrate God's praiseworthy attributes (Our Father who is in heaven, hallowed be Your name.)

- He is Lord (YHWH), holy, and welcoming (v. 1)
- He cares about and produces righteousness and blamelessness in us (v. 2)
- He is a God of truth who brings truth to our very core (v. 2)
- He is a God who transforms our relationships to reflect His character (vv. 3–4)
- He is a God who cares about financial integrity; He is our stability (v. 5)

Prayer Prompts

- I praise You that because of Christ, I can experience intimacy with You, so that . . .
- Because of Your truth, You empower me to speak the truth in my heart, especially when . . .
- I thank You that because of Your [attribute], You have transformed my relationship with . . .

RESPONSE – Surrender to Him and His ways
(Your kingdom come. Your will be done, on earth as it is in heaven.)

- Because I want to be blameless, do the right thing, and speak truth in my heart, I surrender to You and Your will, especially in my struggle with . . .

REQUESTS – Ask the Spirit to guide your prayer over concerns, resources, and relationships

(Give us this day our daily bread. And forgive us our debts, as we also have forgiven our debtors.)

- Give me grace today to restrain my tongue when I talk about . . . [name or situation].
- Give me grace to do good and not evil today in my interactions with . . .
- Give me grace to keep my commitments, especially in my relationship with . . .
- Give me grace today to honor You in how I spend and make my money, especially when . . . (As a visual reminder, take out your wallet or money clip and surrender it to the Lord.)

READINESS – Encouragement and strength for spiritual battle (And do not lead us into temptation, but deliver us from evil.)

- By Your truth and power, strengthen me to be "unshaken" today, especially as I encounter . . .

Acknowledgments

My personal Psalm 15 journey has spanned many years and various places. In reflecting on the impact of this psalm in my walk with Christ, I need to say "thank you" to those who have helped me grow in my desire and determination for an unshaken life.

Rosemary, your selfless partnership and gracious support as my life's mate for over forty years has kept me grounded in countless ways. You have stood by me in the storms, prayed for me in my weakness, and walked with me in twists and turns of our ministry road. You continue to intercede and invest in our children and grandchildren, giving your all in the hopes that they will remain unshaken. I love you and thank God for you.

I am indebted to the treasured saints in three congregations where I have pastored, taught, and applied the principles of Psalm 15. Thank you for listening, responding, and helping to reinforce my understanding of these truths over three decades. (Venture Church, Los Gatos, CA; Arcade Church, Sacramento, CA; and Grace Church, Eden Prairie, MN.)

The board of Strategic Renewal has provided profound support and wisdom over the last twenty years of life and ministry. Thanks for supporting our shared vision and allowing me the freedom to write, speak, coach, and lead the ministry. I am grateful for each of you—Jim Maxim, Joel Archer, Ann Wong-Chan, Josh Stamm, Bill Molinari, Alice Moss, Tim Tyannikov, Mike Mitchener, Brad Thompson, and Tim Wilkins. Special thanks to Tony Brown who has served so selflessly as chairman, staff member, and board member. You are all treasured friends.

Strategic Renewal staff team—you are amazing. I am inspired by your passion for the ministry and the unity we enjoy as we labor together. Each of you brings such unique gifts to our shared work— Carley Phelps, Dennis Henderson, Len Crowley, Ricky Cassford, Justin Jeppeson, John Myers, Tracy Adams, Amber Doggett, Christa Henderson, Heather Rea, Sally Hahn, Todd Bright, and the Bright Team. Thank you for making it all possible through your devotion to Christ and His calling on our lives.

The team at Moody Publishers has encouraged me in countless ways. Thank you for your dedication in guiding and supporting so many authors in your mission to distribute relevant, biblical teaching. I am truly humbled to be counted as one of those writers and have been blessed by the partnership with Duane Sherman, Drew Dyck, and Connor Sterchi.

Supremely, I thank you, Lord Jesus, for the grace that called me to place my faith in Your unwavering promise of abundant life. I am overwhelmed by the daily privilege of building my life upon the Rock of Your truth and faithful provision. I long to see You in the fullness of Your glory—for all of eternity, offering unhindered praise for the fulfillment of Your promise of an unshaken life.

Notes

Introduction: Stirred, Not Shaken

Epigraph: Wayne Martindale and Jerry Root, *The Quotable Lewis* (Wheaton, IL: Tyndale House, 1989), 209. Cited from C. S. Lewis, *Mere Christianity*, 163.

1. https://en.wikipedia.org/wiki/Mount_St._Helens.

2. Ibid.

3. Ibid.

4. https://en.wikipedia.org/wiki/Shaken,_not_stirred.

5. https://www.thefreedictionary.com/stirred.

Chapter One: The Stories of Our Unsettled Lives

Epigraph: Alan Redpath, *The Making of a Man of God* (Westwood, NJ: Fleming H. Revell Co., 1962), 5.

1. "Roosevelt Says, 'Old Ship of State Is On Same Course,'" *New York Times*, March 5, 1938.

2. Charles R. Swindoll, *David: A Man of Passion and Destiny* (Nashville: Thomas Nelson, 2000), 398–99.

3. Carl Friedrich Keil and Franz Delitzsch, *Commentary on the Old Testament*, vol. 5 (Peabody, MA: Hendrickson, 1996), 131.

4. Eugene Merrill, *Kingdom of Priests: A History of Old Testament Israel* (Grand Rapids, MI: Baker Book House, 1987), 243–45.

5. Some commentators place Psalm 15 at the time when the ark was initially moved to Jerusalem, but David's insistence on returning it to the holy hill where it resided would argue against this chronology.

6. Swindoll, *David*, 399.

7. See https://store.strategicrenewal.com/products/praying-the-psalms.

Chapter Two: Our Quest Starts with Questions

Epigraph: Christopher Ash, *Trusting God in the Darkness: A Guide to Understanding the Book of Job* (Wheaton, IL: Crossway, 2021), 62.

1. Diana Cameron, "Kids and Questions," Early Childhood Professional, https://earlychildhoodprofessional.com/kids-questions/.

2. Ibid.

3. Clare Loewenthal, "Five Reasons You Should Never Stop Asking: 'Why?,'" Medium, February 3, 2020, https://medium.com/the-ascent/five-reasons-you-should-never-stop-asking-why-11594b6cc44c.

4. https://www.blueletterbible.org/study/parallel/paral18.cfm

5. "If David is the author, and there is no reason for doubting it, then this Psalm belongs to the time of the rebellion under Absalom, and this supposition is confirmed on every hand." Carl Friedrich Keil and Franz Delitzsch, *Commentary on the Old Testament*, vol. 5 (Peabody, MA: Hendrickson, 1996), 207.

6. "The prayer takes the form of an intercession for God's anointed; for the poet is among the followers of David, the banished one." Keil and Delitzsch, *Commentary on the Old Testament*, 562.

7. Ash, *Trusting God in the Darkness*, 63.

8. Peter C. Craigie, *Word Biblical Commentary*, vol. 19, Psalms 1–50 (Nashville: Thomas Nelson, 2004), 150.

9. Craig C. Broyles, *New International Biblical Commentary*, Psalms (Peabody, MA: Hendrickson Publishers), 91–92.

10. Quoted in J. J. Stewart Perowne, *The Book of Psalms*, vol. 1 (Grand Rapids, MI: Zondervan, 1966), 187.

11. John Calvin, *Commentary on the Book of Psalms*, vol. 1 (Edinburgh: Calvin Translation Society, 1845), 203.

Chapter Three: Straw, Sticks, and Solid Bricks

Epigraph: Stephen L. Carter, *Integrity* (New York: Harper Collins, 1997), 6.

1. Derek Kidner, *Psalms 1–72: An Introduction and Commentary*, vol. 15, Tyndale Old Testament Commentaries (Downers Grove, IL: InterVarsity Press, 1973), 98.

2. Allen P. Ross, "Psalms," in *The Bible Knowledge Commentary: An Exposition of the Scriptures*, vol. 1, ed. J. F. Walvoord and R. B. Zuck (Wheaton, IL: Victor Books, 1985), 803.

3. Carter, *Integrity*, 7.

4. "10 Quotes from Billy Graham on Integrity," The Billy Graham Library, February 13, 2021, https://billygrahamlibrary.org/blog-10-quotes-from-billy-graham-on-integrity/.

5. Carter, *Integrity*, 7.

6. "10 Quotes from Billy Graham on Integrity," Billy Graham Library.

7. "Compartmentalization," *APA Dictionary of Psychology*, American Psychological Association, 2020, https://dictionary.apa.org/compartmentalization.

8. Kirby Anderson, *Dallas Times Herald*, September 23, 1966, https://probe.org/integrity/#text2.

9. "The description applies well to the Absolomites. They are hypocrites, who, now that they have agreed together in their faithless and bloody counsel, have thrown off their disguise and are won over by bribery to their new master; for Absolom had stolen the hearts of the men of Israel." Carl Friedrich Keil

and Franz Delitzsch, *Commentary on the Old Testament*, vol. 5 (Peabody, MA: Hendrickson, 1996), 222.

10. "The prayer takes the form of an intercession for God's anointed; for the poet is among the followers of David, the banished one." Keil and Delitzsch, *Commentary on the Old Testament*, 562.

Chapter Four: The Reassurance of Right Living

Epigraph: Malcolm Guite, "Two New Poems in My Corona on the Psalms: 'The Fool' and 'The Holy Hill,'" June 2, 2020, https://malcolmguite.wordpress.com /2020/06/02two-new-poems-in-my-corona-on-the-psalms-the-fool-and-the-holy-hill/.

1. Keil and Delitzsch argue that Psalm 143 was "certainly composed as coming out of the situation of him who was persecuted by Absalom. The Psalms of this time of persecution are distinguished from those of the time of the persecution by Saul by the deep melancholy into which the mourning of the dethroned king was turned by blending with the penitential sorrowfulness of one conscious of his own guilt." Carl Friedrich Keil and Franz Delitzsch, *Commentary on the Old Testament*, vol. 5 (Peabody, MA: Hendrickson, 1996), 828–29.

2. K. A. Mathews, *Genesis 11:27–50:26*, vol. 1B, The New American Commentary (Nashville: Broadman & Holman Publishers, 2005), 166.

3. Walter Henrichsen, *Thoughts from the Diary of a Desperate Man* (El Cajon, CA: Leadership Foundation, 1999), 126.

4. As updated and cited by professor David Brionies, https://www.desiringgod .org/articles/dressed-in-his-righteousness-alone#fnref3.

5. Charles Spurgeon, *Spurgeon at His Best*, comp. Tom Carter (Grand Rapids, MI: Baker, 1988), 178.

6. John Trent and Rick Hicks, *Seeking Solid Ground: Anchoring Your Life in Godly Character* (Colorado Springs, CO: Focus on the Family, 1995), 71.

7. Dane Ortlund, "Reflections on Handling the Old Testament as Jesus Would Have Us: Psalm 15 as a Case Study," *Themelios* 42, no. 1 (2017): 86–87.

Chapter Five: The Epicenter of Authenticity

Epigraph: Dietrich Bonhoeffer, *Meditating on the Word* (Lanham, MD: Rowman & Littlefield, 2000), 50.

1. https://www.studylight.org/commentaries/eng/dcc/2-samuel-11.html.

2. John Owen, *Works of John Owen, Volume VI* (Edinburgh: Banner of Truth, 1987), 92.

3. John Trent and Rick Hicks, *Seeking Solid Ground: Anchoring Your Life in Godly Character* (Colorado Springs: Focus on the Family, 1995), 77.

4. Wayne Grudem, *Christian Ethics: An Introduction to Biblical Moral Reasoning* (Wheaton, IL: Crossway, 2018), 332.

5. Attributed to Isaac of Ninevah.

Chapter Six: Keeping Your Lips from Sinking Ships

Epigraph: Edward Reyner, *Rules for Government of the Tongue* (London: Printed by R. I. for Thomas Newberry, 1656), 105. Cited in I. D. E. Thomas, *A Puritan Golden Treasury* (Edinburgh: The Banner of Truth Trust, 2000), 296.

1. Jon Bloom, "Lay Aside the Weight of Slander," Desiring God, December 19, 2015, https://www.desiringgod.org/articles/lay-aside-the-weight-of-slander.

2. Cited by P. Ellingworth, "Malice," in *New Bible Dictionary*, ed. D. R. W. Wood et al. (Downers Grove, IL: InterVarsity Press, 1996), 720.

3. Quoted by his son, Gavin Ortlund, "3 Ways to Respond When Slandered," The Gospel Coalition, October 21, 2016, https://www.thegospelcoalition.org/article/3-ways-to-respond-when-slandered/.

4. John Piper, "'Rejoice When You Are Slandered': How to Do the Humanly Impossible," Bethlehem College & Seminary Chapel, Minneapolis, Desiring God, July 25, 2021, https://www.desiringgod.org/messages/rejoice-when-you-are-slandered.

Chapter Seven: Defying Evil, Doing Good

Epigraph: Watchman Nee, *Not I But Christ: Basic Lesson Series, Volume 4* (New York: Christian Fellowship Publishers, 1974), 67–68.

1. John Trent and Rick Hicks, *Seeking Solid Ground: Anchoring Your Life in Godly Character* (Colorado Springs, CO: Focus on the Family, 1995), 122.

2. John M. Dawson and Patrick A. Langan, "Murder in Families," Bureau of Justice Statistics, July 1994, https://bjs.ojp.gov/content/pub/pdf/mf.pdf.

3. Nee, *Not I But Christ*, 64.

4. Gene Edwards, *A Tale of Three Kings: A Study in Brokenness* (Auburn, ME: Christian Books, 1980), 34–35.

Chapter Eight: Stop the Spread

Epigraph: Ziad K. Abdelnour, *Economic Warfare: Secrets of Wealth Creation in the Age of Welfare Politics* (Indianapolis: Wiley Publishers, 2011), 23.

1. https://en.wikipedia.org/wiki/Chinese_whispers.

2. Paul Tripp, "Do You Love Controversy?," PaulTripp.com, February 8, 2023, https://www.paultripp.com/wednesdays-word/posts/do-you-love-controversy.

3. Ira Hyman, "The Unshakeable Power of Rumor," *Psychology Today*, January 28, 2016, https://www.psychologytoday.com/us/blog/mental-mishaps/201601/the-unshakeable-power-rumor.

4. https://englishaesop.blogspot.com/2010/09/herford-four-bulls-and-lion.html.

5. https://firefighterinsider.com/how-fast-does-fire-spread/.

6. Randall Yip, "How the Lahaina Fire Spread So Quickly," AsAmNews, August 18, 2023, https://asamnews.com/2023/08/18/how-the-lahaina-fire-spread-so-quickly/.

7. Kiara Alfonseca, "Latest Out of Maui: Residents Prepare for Their Return to Lahaina," ABC News, September 18, 2023, https://abcnews.go.com/US/latest-maui-recovery-rebuilding-begins-after-deadly-wildfires/story?id=102929475#:~:text=The%20death%20toll%20stands%20at%20115.%20Of%20the,be%20reached%20by%20authorities.%20Fifty-six%20people%20remain%20unidentified.

8. Jon Bloom, "Lay Aside the Weight of Slander," Desiring God, December 19, 2015, https://www.desiringgod.org/articles/lay-aside-the-weight-of-slander.

9. Edwards P. Sri, "The Feathers of Gossip: How Our Words Can Build Up or Tear Down," Catholic Education Resource Center, https://www.catholiceducation.org/en/religion-and-philosophy/philosophy/the-feathers-of-gossip-how-our-words-can-build-up-or-tear-down.html.

10. Anna Kaufman, "Trump's Claims on Declassification Spark Confusion. What Are the Types of 'Classified' Documents?," *USA Today*, August 15, 2022, https://www.usatoday.com/story/news/2022/08/15/classified-documents-top-secret-explained/10328931002/.

Chapter Nine: Godliness by Association

Epigraph: As quoted by Fred Smith, *You and Your Network: Getting the Most Out of Life* (Waco, TX: Word Publishers, 1984), 186.

1. Described in detail in my book, *The Deeper Life: Satisfying the 8 Vital Longings of the Soul* (Minneapolis: Baker House, 2014), 237–38. (Available at store.strategicrenewal.com.)

2. Smith, *You and Your Network*, 68.

3. Ibid., 80–81.

4. Morris Massey, *The People Puzzle* (Reston, VA: Reston Publishing Co., 1979), part 3.

5. https://www.grimmstories.com/en/grimm_fairy-tales/the_old_man_and_his_grandson.

6. I use a helpful app called 2nd Vote (https://www.2ndvote.com/company-scores/). I know there are other good resources.

7. Crawford Loritts, Strategic Renewal Global Symposium, September 13, 2022, https://vimeo.com/750426557.

Chapter Ten: The Power of a Promise Keeper

Epigraph: Heidi Tai, "The Power of Promise Keeping in a 'Maybe' World: Reflections from 1917," The Gospel Coalition Australia, February 20, 2020, https://au.thegospelcoalition.org/article/the-power-of-promise-keeping-in-a-maybe-world-reflections-from-1917/.

1. John P. Bartkowski, "Whatever Happened to the Promise Keepers?," http://hirr.hartsem.edu/research/religion_family_pksummary.html.

2. "Lying Motivations: Exploring Personality Correlates of Lying and Motivations to Lie," *Canadian Journal of Behavioural Science* 54, no. 4 (2022): 335–40, https://psycnet.apa.org/record/2022-44652-001.

3. Arash Emamzadeh, "Research Reveals the Most Common Reasons People Lie," Psychology Today, December 21, 2022, https://www.psychologytoday.com/us/blog/finding-a-new-home/202207/research-reveals-the-most-common-reasons-people-lie.

4. For example, Samuel deceived Saul into believing that he was going to Bethlehem to offer a sacrifice when in reality, he went to anoint one of Jesse's sons (David) to replace Saul as king (1 Sam. 16:2). The Hebrew midwives lied to Pharoah to protect Hebrew baby boys (Ex. 1:15–21). David lied to the priest Ahimelech about his intentions while fleeing for his life (1 Sam. 21:1–6). The prostitute Rahab lied to protect Joshua's spies (Josh. 2:1–7). Despite these examples, the biblical commands against lying are clear.

5. Douglas J. Moo, *The Letter of James: An Introduction and Commentary*, vol. 16, Tyndale New Testament Commentaries (Downers Grove, IL: InterVarsity Press, 1985), 179.

Chapter Eleven: Why Money Matters

Epigraph: John Piper, "Magnifying God with Money," Desiring God, December 14, 1997, https://www.desiringgod.org/messages/magnifying-god-with-money.

1. "Money Ruining Marriages in America: A Ramsey Solutions Study," Ramsey Solutions, February 6, 2018, https://www.ramseysolutions.com/company/newsroom/releases/money-ruining-marriages-in-america.

2. Jesse Wisnewski, "Bible Verses About Money: 9 Biblical Principles of Money & Possessions," Tithe.ly, May 29, 2020, https://get.tithe.ly/blog/bible-verses-about-money.

3. Attributed to Richard Halverson in Randy Alcorn, *Money, Possessions, and Eternity* (Carol Stream, IL: Tyndale, 2003), 3.

4. Nik Popli, "Credit Card Debt Just Hit an All-Time High. Here's How You Can Pay It Down," *Time*, February 17, 2023, https://time.com/6256336/credit-card-debt-how-to-pay-off/.

5. Stella Chan and Ray Sanchez, "Nun Admits to Stealing Over $835,000 from Her School to Help Finance Gambling Habit, Feds Say," CNN, June 10, 2021, https://www.cnn.com/2021/06/10/us/nun-school-embezzlement-gambling/index.html.

6. Kenneth Garger, "Pennsylvania Church Treasurer Accused of Stealing $150K to Fuel Porn Addiction," March 11, 2021, *New York Post*, https://nypost.com/2021/03/11/pa-church-treasurer-accused-of-stealing-150k-to-fuel-porn-addiction/.

7. *Merriam-Webster*, s.v. "bribe (*n.*)," last updated August 25, 2023, https://www.merriam-webster.com/dictionary/bribe.

8. Andrew Reid, "FIFA World Cup in Qatar Rocked by $6 Million Bribery Scandal," November 10, 2022, https://au.sports.yahoo.com/fifa-world-cup-2022-qatar-official-rocked-six-million-dollar-bribery-allegations-000024963.html.

9. Ian Ward, "The Many, Many Controversies Surrounding the 2022 World Cup, Explained," *Vox*, November 19, 2022, https://www.vox.com/world/23450515/world-cup-fifa-qatar-2022-controversy-scandals-explained.

10. Ajai Prakash, "Radio Personality Paul Harvey Tells the Story Of . . . ," SermonCentral, February 25, 2009, https://www.sermoncentral.com/sermon-illustrations/71310/radio-personality-paul-harvey-tells-the-story-of-by-ajai-prakash.

Conclusion: The Promising Playlist of the Heart

Epigraph: Dave Keesling, *A Journey: Life in Real Time* (Woodland Park, CO: Dave Keesling Productions, 2007), 174.

1. Robert J. Morgan, *My All in All: Daily Assurance of God's Grace* (Nashville: Broadman and Holman, 2008), February 26.

Appendix One: Salvation: The Beginning Place for a Never-Shaken Life

1. Adapted from "What Is the Plan of Salvation?," GotQuestions.org, last updated January 4, 2022, https://www.gotquestions.org/plan-of-salvation.html; and "What Is Repentance and Is It Necessary for Salvation?," GotQuestions.org, last updated January 4, 2022, https://www.gotquestions.org/repentance.html.

MARK SAYERS SHOWS HOW CHRISTIANS CAN OFFER A NON-ANXIOUS PRESENCE IN A VOLATILE WORLD.

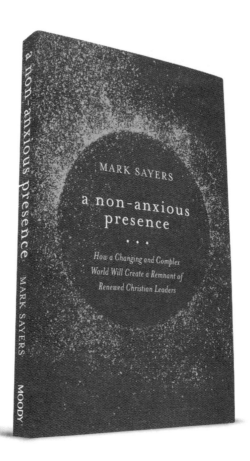

MOODY
Publishers®

From the Word to Life®

Crisis is a great revealer. It knocks us off our thrones. It uncovers weaknesses and brings to light idols. Yet amid the chaos of a crisis comes opportunity. Crisis always precedes renewal. See how that renewal happens—churches and leaders discover strategic ways to see our culture changed for Christ.

Also available as an eBook and an audiobook

EXPERIENCE GOD THROUGH A CRISIS—
AND THROUGH PRAYER

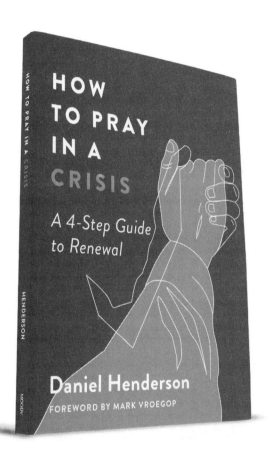

**MOODY
Publishers®**

From the Word to Life®

How to Pray in a Crisis outlines how God can use a crisis to draw His people near to Him. This four-step guide will help you understand the nature of prayer and how it can lead to spiritual renewal in your life. Learn to pray with conviction, competency, community, and in a way that inspires others.

Also available as an eBook and an audiobook